GARDEN ROOMS AND GREENHOUSES

(Morley Baer)

GARDEN ROOMS AND GREENHOUSES

by Jack Kramer

HARPER & ROW, PUBLISHERS

New York, Evanston, San Francisco, London

1817

Drawings by Adrián Martínez, unless otherwise noted.

Plant lists in Chapters 5 and 10 are from *Flowering and Foliage House Plants* (Fawcett Publications) by Jack Kramer.

The photographs by Morley Baer are used by permission of *House & Garden,* copyright © 1972 by The Condé Nast Publications Inc.

FIRST EDITION

STANDARD BOOK NUMBER: 06-012459-8

LIBRARY OF CONGRESS CATALOG CARD NUMBER: 72-77754

Contents

Color illustrations are found facing pages 36, 37, 52, 53, 68, 69, 84, and 85.

Acknowledgments

This book has evolved over a three-year period (or, more likely, it goes back ten years, to when I built my first garden room). In this span of time I have met many gardeners from many parts of the country who had, or were building, places for plants. It is impossible to thank each and every one who helped me along the way. I hope they understand my not listing names but just offering a big thank you to all concerned.

I also owe thanks to several architects and interior designers whose work is included in this book and who shared my enthusiasm for the greenhouse–garden room project. These include John Laile, who graciously assisted me with technical data for Chapter 2 of this book; Ira Kurlander, architect; Bob Overstreet, architect; Brock Arms, architect; and Andrew R. Addkison, interior designer.

Other people who deserve thanks for performing the painstaking tasks of going through photo files and searching out garden rooms to photograph are Max Eckert, photographer, of Los Angeles; Hedrich Blessing, photographer, of Chicago; and Joyce R. Wilson, photographer, of Mill Valley, California.

Special thanks again to my artist, Adrián Martínez, interior designer, whose original designs are used in this book.

Finally, I wish to thank my publishers, Harper & Row of New York, for their splendid assistance in this project, especially Cass Canfield, Jr., who shared my enthusiasm for what we fondly call the new room of the home . . . the garden room.

JACK KRAMER

Introduction:
A Place for Plants and People

The style of architecture in the houses of today is far removed from that of the houses of twenty years ago. And the greenhouse is no longer the separate, sealed glass chamber of the 1890s. New trends, new designs, and a new way of living have transformed the greenhouse into the extra room, an integral part of the home designated at various times by various names—garden room, plant room, atrium, solarium, conservatory, outdoor room. And although it is still a place for plants, it has become a place for people, too. What is more pleasant than to have morning coffee, surrounded by greenery, or to read a book in the charming atmosphere of a greenhouse–garden room?

The conventional freestanding greenhouse is still with us, and certainly has its purposes, but even these structures are changing. Today there is an array of new designs, including ones for round and ones for hexagonal units, radically different from the metal-and-glass greenhouses of yesterday. The new attached greenhouse–garden room offers limitless possibilities for recreational living, whether it is used as a sitting room, a dining retreat, or simply as a lavish display of greenery.

The garden room takes the greenhouse a step further. Generally, it has a partial ceiling of glass or plastic to admit natural light. It is designed to blend with the architecture of the home, and, more often than not, it is the place where the family spends most of its time. It can be large and dramatic, accented with giant plants and Plexiglas domes, or it can be casual and small, with houseplants and modular skylights. But no matter what it is, filled with green plants it offers an inviting change of scenery for the homeowner.

The garden room is a place to enjoy all year. It is well-designed, pleasing to see from the outside and equally pleasant inside, with bright colors, handsome furniture, and attractive plants. Here is a segment of nature at our fingertips, convenient to the house and a convenience to the family as well.

This is the first book to explore new greenhouse styles and the new space in the home—the Garden Room. And it is not only a book about garden rooms and greenhouses; it also contains information on what kind of plants to grow, how to place them for maximum effect, how to take care of them, and where to find them.

I hope this book will be helpful to the gardener who wants a place for plants and wants to bring the outdoors indoors, as well as furnish inspiration and enthusiasm for innovative garden room design among architects and interior designers.

GARDEN ROOMS AND GREENHOUSES

(Morley Baer)

CHAPTER 1

The Garden Room

In the last decade we have tried more and more to bring the outdoors indoors. This means using living plants of all kinds to provide natural beauty indoors. In our quest to bring nature to us, we have turned the extra room—the recreation room or rumpus room—into a garden area. Sometimes only a few plants are used, while in other situations the room becomes a tropical paradise.

The garden room is not new. In Grandmother's day it was called a sunroom or a solarium. Of course, today's garden room is somewhat different from yesterday's sunroom or solarium because of architectural changes and different modes of living. Nor is the garden room generally a tacked-on addition, the result of an afterthought; it is usually an integral part of the home. However, it can be equally attractive when added to an existing structure and intelligently decorated: the room is treated as if it were a garden and the garden as if it were a room.

Whether the garden room is professionally designed or a do-it-yourself project, it is still, of course, decorated with plants. Small trees in handsome tubs can be placed in strategic corners, or in islands, to break the monotony of the room and to guide traffic. Smaller potted plants and possibly some garden furniture can be used to complete the picture. The greenery can be in the center of the house (atrium), where it can be viewed from most rooms; adjacent to the dining or living room; or an extension of an existing area, such as a porch. It can even be a porch converted to a garden room, generally less expensive than the other types of rooms mentioned (but not much). But however it is decorated or where it is located, this room is a place where living plants complement everyday activities.

My own first garden room was a solarium in a 1930-type Chicago apartment twenty minutes from downtown Chicago. There were large windows and a tile floor, and although there was no top light (skylight or dome), dozens of plants thrived. In California, on a site that was originally a concrete aggregate terrace, I built a redwood and glass structure with skylights for my indoor plants. In my new house, the garden room is just recently completed. It has a brick floor, is two stories high to accommodate tall plants, and has clerestory windows rather than skylights.

The kind of garden room you choose depends on the house itself, the uses for the extra room, and just how much indoor greenery you want. In any case, the garden room will add value to your home, as well as attractiveness.

Although we used to think of Florida as the location for a room for plants (Florida room), today indoor greenery appears in all homes and in all climates. The design of the garden room is limited only by your imagination, but remember that, basically, natural materials—wood, stone, brick—should be used.

An architect may not realize, at first, what you want when you ask him to design a place for plants; his first thought may be that you want a greenhouse or hothouse. This is exactly what you do *not* want, since the greenhouse is solely a place for plants; the garden room is for people and plants. Furthermore, it is not a room completely glass enclosed; if it were, it would be too hot for plants and people (all greenhouses must be shaded

Large sculptural plants—*Dracaena marginata, Dizygotheca elegantissima, Ficus lyrata*—are the focal points of this handsome garden room. The floor is hand-hewn tile, the ceiling curved Plexiglas, and the seasonal potted plants complete the exciting picture.

(Hedrich-Blessing)

in summer from intense heat). Most importantly, the garden room should be in character with the architecture of and convenient to the house.

Basically, the garden room has:

A floor impervious to water
A ceiling that admits 40 percent natural light
Adequate windows for ventilation
Places for plants
Electrical outlets
Water outlets
Places for furniture
Drainage facilities

The design of the room can be simple, with a few plastic domes, or it may be elaborate, with hexagonally shaped glass skylights. It may soar two stories with thin vertical lines—an elegant two-story loft is a definite possibility—or be more horizontal in design; roofs may be peaked, domed, or have skylights, and walls may be all glass or partial glass. There are innumerable design variations for garden rooms, and I will show you many different kinds to help guide you to the right extra room for you.

A PLACE FOR PLANTS

Many factors have contributed to the popularity of the garden room—up-to-date heating and humidifying systems, for example—but the most important considerations are the plants themselves. We now know that many plants do not want or need hothouse conditions. Small trees and shrubs now flourish in garden rooms, as do orchids and bromeliads. A whole new kind of gardening has developed in the last decade and, with it, a new knowledge of plants. They are now considered structural elements within a room, and, although large plants may be scattered throughout the house (and should be), the place where plants are en masse is always the most inviting setting because the plants soften the sometimes severe lines of contemporary architecture and make the area agreeable.

Select big plants for big decoration—a palm or a tree-trained oleander. Use specimen plants as focal points in the room and landscape around them with smaller plants. Strive for balance and scale.

There are several ways to accommodate smaller plants in the area. Wooden or glass window shelves are always suitable, as are suspension poles fitted with trays, or, of course, hanging baskets suspended from the ceiling.

Commercial window shelves and brackets are sold at stores, but generally custom units will have to be made. This is not difficult. Even inexpensive angle irons, painted a suitable color, are pleasing as supports for glass shelves. Make shelves wide (about 12 inches) so they can hold a 5- or 6-inch pot. Use ¼-inch crystal or tempered glass so that the shelf will hold the weight of several potted plants. If shelves are more than 28 inches long, brace them at the center with angle irons. Redwood shelves can be used as they come from the lumber house, but they do block out light.

Suspension poles and brackets with redwood trays are excellent for plants. These poles are available at department stores and attach to surfaces with suction cups and spring compressors, thus eliminating the need for bolts in the ceiling and floor. The channels of the poles have slots for adjustable metal brackets. Trays for the plants are a do-it-yourself project. I use 1-inch redwood strips, placed ½ inch apart, nailed on a wooden frame; a 12″ by 12″ tray accommodates a 6-inch pot. The metal brackets hold considerable weight and thus can support heavy plants.

The poles should be placed so they do not block traffic in the room. The size of the room dictates how many to use; decide how much open area you want for seating or walking.

Hanging baskets with plants are understandably popular because plants are thus placed at eye level and can be more fully appreciated. And hanging baskets fill a void near the ceiling that otherwise is simply unused space. And do not overlook the dramatic effect that hanging plants give to a room. They provide a splendid display, and the new clip-on saucers prevent excess water from draining from the pots.

Baskets generally come with chain or rope for hanging. Simply install eye hooks in the ceiling or beams if you want them to hang directly from the ceiling. Wrought-iron brackets are another way to support basket containers. The brackets are wall hung, and the chain fits on the end of the unit.

LOCATION

The garden room can be the focal point of the home, a place to which the eye is immediately drawn, or it can be a smaller, intimate area off a

An old-fashioned garden room is perfect for this house,
complete with ceiling fan and lush ferns.
(Max Eckert photo; Sally Sirkin, Interior Designer)

A latticework ceiling is a perfect foil in a charming
garden room; foliage plants, chrysanthemums, and azaleas
are the plants. Wicker furniture adds country charm to
this inviting room.

(Max Eckert photo; Ron Collier, Interior Designer)

This scale model shows a garden room that is an integral part of the home and, although there are only a few plants, the scene is an attractive one.
(Joyce R. Wilson photo; Adrián Martinez, Interior Designer)

Futuristic and unique, a circular-domed garden room is part of this scale model home. A platform serves as a seating area framed in plants. A glass gallery leads to the room.
(Joyce R. Wilson photo; Adrián Martinez, Interior Designer)

room. It can be large or small, long and narrow, square or rectangular, but its design should always be in keeping with the architecture of the home. The specific location of the room depends on your mode of living: I have seen delightful greeneries off kitchens; a garden room adjacent to a living room offers a broad vista of greenery and makes the living room seem larger; and a garden room off a bedroom can provide dramatic eye interest and charm.

Do not be too concerned about exposures, for there are plants for all kinds of light conditions, and even north areas can become handsome garden rooms. Decide first *where* you want the room and then proceed with appropriate design and selection of the proper plants for that exposure.

A west-orientated garden room is likely to be hot in the afternoon and not as successful for winter use as one with a southern exposure. There will be no morning sun on the west side, but until lunchtime it will be a pleasant morning retreat.

The garden room that faces east will always be cheerful and flooded with morning sun and will cool off in the afternoon. In hot climates it is the choice location.

The sun will always flood a south-facing garden room from morning to dusk, regardless of the season or latitude.

After designing and constructing garden rooms for five different houses in two different climate areas (Chicago and California), I have found that a 16′ by 20′ area will accommodate plants as well as people without crowding. This size greenery should be adjacent to the living or dining room, and not to bedroom or bath. Garden rooms for these intimate areas are generally simply for viewing and growing plants, so they can be somewhat small compared with the garden room of the type we are discussing, which serves a dual function.

It is important to remember that the room with plants, as opposed to a room without greenery, will immediately draw people to it. This is where the guest will most often settle, if there is suitable furniture, so make the room large enough to be comfortable.

COST AND CONSTRUCTION

A garden room can be simple and not exceed $2,000 in price, or it may be elaborate and cost as much as a standard-sized room, that is, about $25 per square foot, depending upon where you live. If you do part of the work yourself, such as carpentry and framing, some money can be saved, of course. However, foundations and flooring generally must be done by professionals, and this service varies in cost from state to state.

Prime consideration must be given to ceilings and floors, for here is where the garden room differs from other rooms in the house. Ceilings should admit some top light; the floor should be impervious to water.

The roof of a garden room should have a glass, fiber glass, or Plexiglas area. If 50 percent of the ceiling admits natural light, you can grow almost any kind of plant. The ceiling design can include a conventional flat skylight, made-to-order Plexiglas domes, or standard-sized modular domes. Four 36-inch-square domes in a 16′ by 20′ room will give sufficient light to grow many plants, and Plexiglas domes are virtually leakproof. The ceiling can also be alternating panels of plywood and flat plastic. But no matter which method you decide to use, do not install a complete glass or plastic ceiling. The room will be too hot for plants—or people. (Greenhouse manufacturers have designs for garden rooms available on request. It would be wise to have this information before hiring an architect to design the room or before you do it yourself.)

For skylight areas, use ¼-inch wire glass or tempered glass (usually required by state building codes), which can either be clear or have a pattern. Patterned glass eliminates about 35 percent of the natural light, but this is still enough light to grow many plants. With any glass skylight, be prepared to have some leakage; I have never seen a waterproof glass skylight.

To save money, choose standard-sized commercial skylight frames of aluminum or galvanized iron. Custom framing for glass—wood or metal—is extremely expensive; although if the roof of the garden room is of a special design (sawtooth or triangular, for instance), custom metal or wooden frames must be made. In any case, whether you use clear or patterned glass, custom-made Plexiglas domes or commercial ones, call in a glazier to do the necessary installation.

Select a waterproof material for the garden room floor. Concrete or concrete aggregate are of course very suitable, since these materials are inexpensive and last a long time. Another appropriate material is tile, which is now being manufactured in many colors, styles, and finishes. In

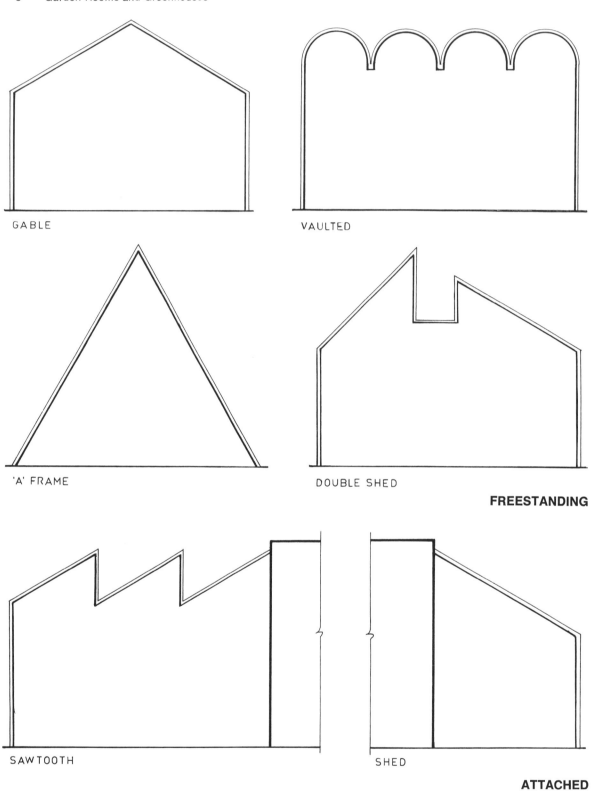

GABLE

VAULTED

'A' FRAME

DOUBLE SHED

FREESTANDING

SAWTOOTH

SHED

ATTACHED

ROOF VARIATIONS

Fig. 1

FLOOR PATTERNS

CONCRETE AND REDWOOD

4 × 4 OR 4 × 6 CIRCUMFERENCE FRAMING
2 × 4 DIVIDER STRIPS
BUILT-IN FLOOR LEVEL PLANTERS

Fig. 2

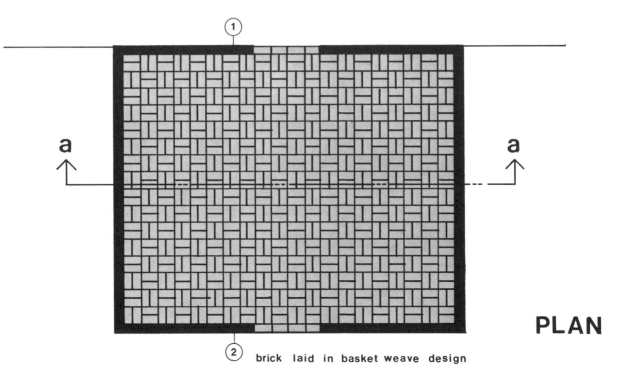

PLAN

brick laid in basket weave design

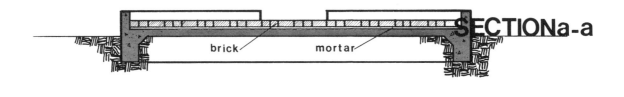

SECTIONa-a

brick   mortar

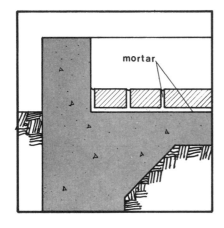

mortar

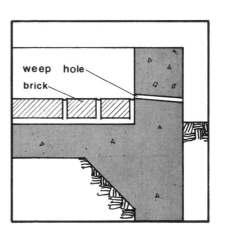

weep hole

brick

DETAILS   ①   ②

BRICK FLOOR

Forrest Liles

Fig. 3

most cases you can lay tile yourself. It is not an easy task, but it can be done in a weekend.

Brick is a handsome flooring material and now comes in several colors and finishes. It is easy to work with, can be installed in many different designs—basket weave, random pattern, and so on —and it is impervious to time. It can be laid on a sand base, with the interstices filled with sand, or it can be put on a concrete slab.

Paving blocks can also be used as a flooring. These are compressed concrete blocks that are uniform in thickness and have straight edges. They come in several pleasing shapes—hexagonal, random, and round—and in many colors. Lay these blocks directly on a sand base. Because the tiles are not held rigidly in place, the cracking that often occurs in a poured-concrete floor is virtually eliminated.

Thin sheets of marble in block sizes are another idea for a garden room floor. Generally more expensive than other materials, marble is indeed handsome.

Do not select just any material for a garden room floor. Choose one that is handsome and will blend with the scheme of the room (see Chapter 2). And if you are doing the job yourself, be sure to allow some facility for drainage. This may be done in one of two ways: you can either slope the floor away from the house or put in suitable drain tiles under the paving.

While not specifically a garden room, this greenery on the side of the home adds great flair to the interior. The lattice ceiling affords perfect light for plants.

(Max Eckert photo; William Chidester, Interior Designer)

CHAPTER 2

Building the Garden Room

Whether you decide to do the garden room yourself or have a designer and/or a contractor do it, some basic information about construction can help you decide about materials and designs. The idea is to provide a place for plants, but you also want a functional room and an aesthetically pleasing structure. Like the many forms of plant life, designs are limited only by your imagination.

Have patience in selecting a final design. Make sketches that show the room size and shape and consider where it joins the house. Pay attention to such details as doors, so there is easy entrance and exit from the home, and study exposures so there will be adequate light for plants.

Be sure foundations and footings conform to the local building codes, and that the walls and floors are made of materials to withstand the humidity and moisture necessary in an indoor greenery. Do not forget to include water outlets at convenient places (it's a bother to transport water from kitchen to plants) and remember that floors must have drains to carry off excess water. Electricity should also be provided, for a garden room is a special delight at night. Although these installations are all jobs for the professional, it is wise to have some knowledge of their workings so you can talk intelligently to plumbers and electricians.

The following information is rudimentary and not to be considered comprehensive; however, I hope it will provide some basic knowledge of construction details so that you will know what to ask for when talking to contractors or carpenters.

FLOORING

Give serious thought to the kind of flooring and design of the floor that will be in the garden room. Dripping water on floors is a nuisance, so select tile or brick or other impervious materials that can tolerate waterspill without harm. Since the garden room is generally adjacent to the house it is wise to choose flooring complementary to the home. Hand-hewn tiles are expensive but elegant; brick is always a desirable choice, for it looks good in almost any setting; and different kinds of concrete aggregate are also pleasing. Wood has its uses, too, for it is easy to clean and to install. (See drawing 4.)

Be sure a moisture membrane is installed underneath the concrete pad to prevent dampness rising from the ground from going through the flooring. A 30-pound roofing felt overlapped 4 to 6 inches is satisfactory. (See drawing 5.)

To lay a poured slab concrete floor with aggregate finish, use the following procedure:

1. Encircle the room with 4 by 4s (4 by 6s are also satisfactory), keeping a level line with a carpenter's level.

2. Crisscross the floor with 2 by 4s (stringers) to create a pattern.

3. When nailing the 2 by 4s to the 4 by 4 perimeter, use the toenail method of adjoining two pieces of lumber so no nails will show when the project is completed.

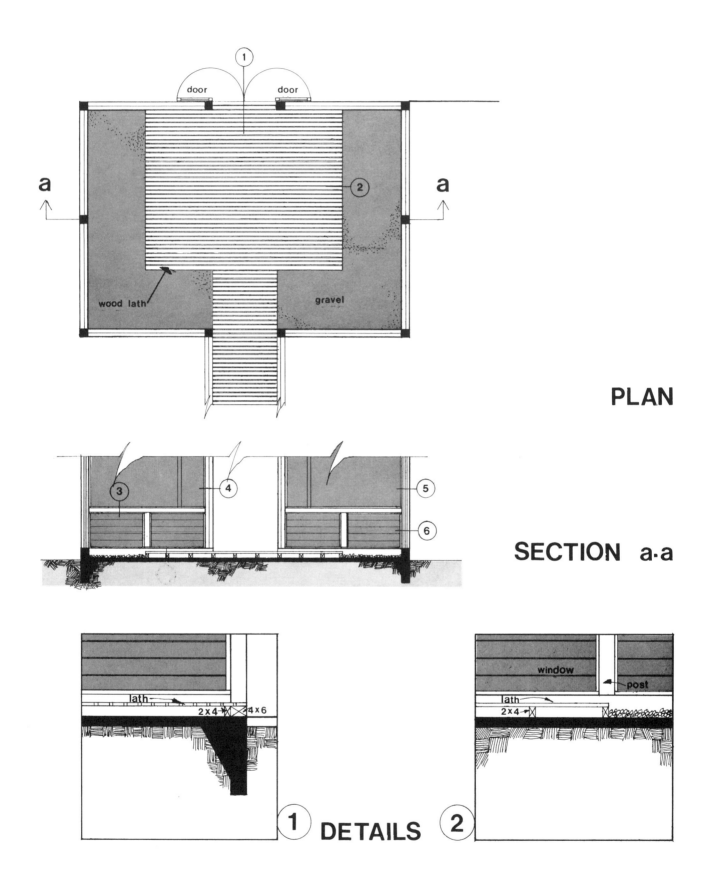

PLAN

SECTION a·a

DETAILS

WOOD LATH FLOOR

Forrest Liles

Fig. 4

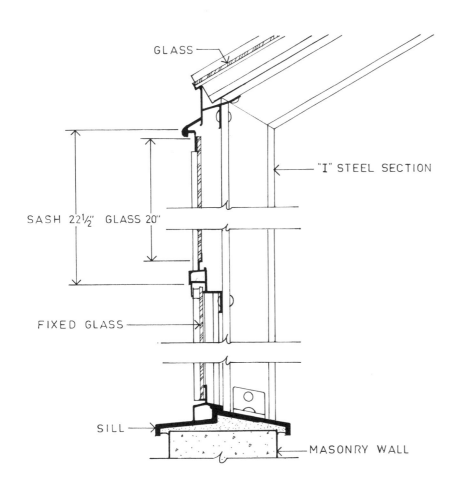

GLASS

"I" STEEL SECTION

SASH 22½" GLASS 20"

FIXED GLASS

SILL

MASONRY WALL

GREENHOUSE SASH DETAIL

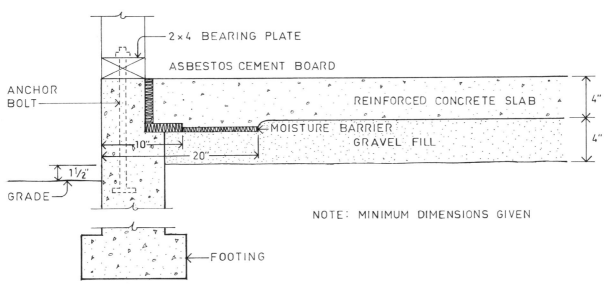

2 × 4 BEARING PLATE

ASBESTOS CEMENT BOARD

ANCHOR BOLT

REINFORCED CONCRETE SLAB

4"

MOISTURE BARRIER

GRAVEL FILL

4"

10"

20"

1½"

GRADE

NOTE: MINIMUM DIMENSIONS GIVEN

FOOTING

SLAB ON GRADE FOUNDATION

Fig. 5

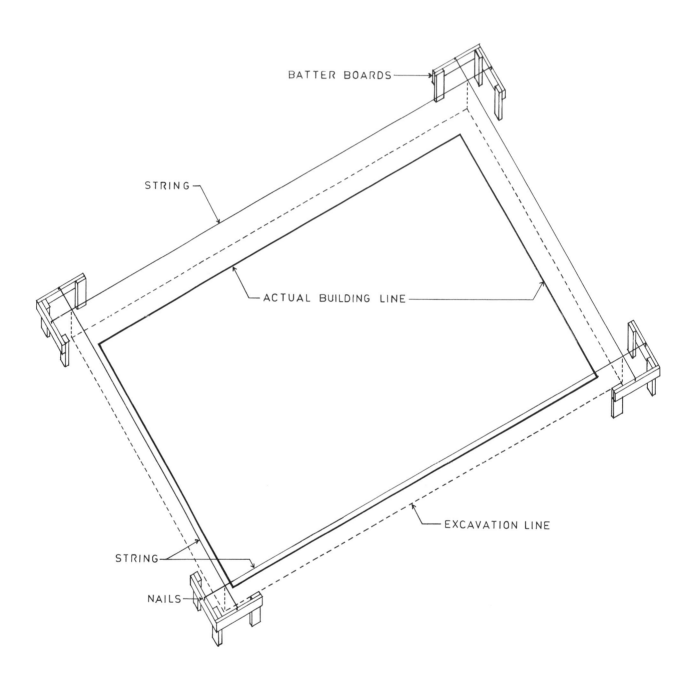

BATTER BOARDS

STRING

ACTUAL BUILDING LINE

EXCAVATION LINE

STRING

NAILS

FOUNDATIONS

Fig. 6

4. To be sure the 2 by 4 stringers are straight, measure and mark the desired distances on the 4 by 4s and place a small nail at each marking. Then stretch a string from one nail to the other where the 2 by 4s are to be placed.

5. Place large 5-inch nails about every 18 inches along the sides of both the 2 by 4s and the 4 by 4s, pounding them in about one-fourth of their length. This will give the aggregate something to adhere to when it sets up and will keep the wood stringers and concrete from separating if there is any ground settling.

TO INSTALL A FOOTING

1. Drive 12 stakes or 4 batter boards 4 to 8 feet from the prospective dividing corners of the desired design. Then, using string, lay out the exact plan of the building from stake to stake or board to board. (See drawing 6.)

2. Dig a trench around the desired circumference of the proposed site. Make the trench approximately 2 feet wide and a minimum of 1 foot deep (or whatever local building codes advise).

3. Once you have decided on the height of the foundation footing, use a level to be certain all batter boards or stakes are on the same level. (*Note:* If possible, leave 3-inch holes in the base of the foundation about every 6 feet so water can run off to a lower grade. The drainpipe should extend all around the exterior of the room at the base of the footing in the trench.)

4. Foundation framing equipment is usually available on a rental basis. If not, use ¾-inch plywood to frame the foundation. The width of the footing should be 8 inches (or whatever local building codes require).

5. If your garden room is a heavy structure, reinforce footings with steel rods laid horizontally and vertically within the footing. Pound the vertical rods in the ground between the foundation framing and then, using wires, tie the horizontal rods to the vertical ones.

6. Leave ¼ to ½ inch "D" anchor bolts (available at lumberyards) protruding from the top of the footing so there will be a base for nailing in upright members. The length of the bolt depends on the size of the bearing plate you use, but be sure to allow for a longer bolt rather than a short one.

The bearing plate should be laid approximately 1 inch inside the outside line of the footing.

7. Apply mastic to the top of the footing in order to stop capillary action.

TO INSTALL DRAIN TILES

1. As I've mentioned, be sure there is an adequate drainage system placed at the base of and through the foundation or under the slab to carry off excess water.

2. For outside drainage, place the drain tiles at the base and through the footings, on 4 to 6 inches of rough gravel.

3. For inside drainage, plan a floor drain. Before the floor is installed, locate the drainage heads in a low area of the flooring.

WALLS

Because garden rooms need a good deal of light so plants will grow well, you will probably not want solid walls, but the main structural members, of course, must be in place. Structural members may be placed between the glass panes on 32-inch centers. The members themselves may be many different sizes, depending on the design, height, and support needed for the roof.

The facing for the exterior walls should be compatible with the extremes of dampness and heat in your climate, and, although glass is most commonly used for walls, there are replacements, such as Denverlite, a fiber glass that emits light but is resistant to wind and hail. Do not consider Thermopane for walls; it costs a great deal more than standard glass and is only necessary in extreme weather conditions. Glass or plastic can be sealed with caulking compounds and glazing putty; preformed rubber moldings can be used on aluminum casements. (See drawing 7.)

Be sure to include electrical conduits and water pipes in the wall design.

Many types of prefabricated doors and window frames of wood or metal are available at local lumberyards.

The general practice in framing doors and windows is to use either 4 by 6s or 4 by 8s, depending on the span above the door and window.

Framing being set for concrete aggregate floor.
(Joyce R. Wilson)

Poured concrete aggregate floor; note bolts for walls.
(Joyce R. Wilson)

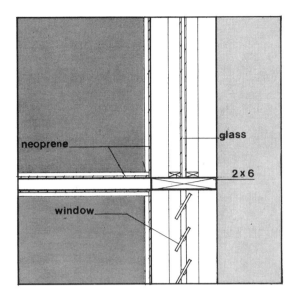

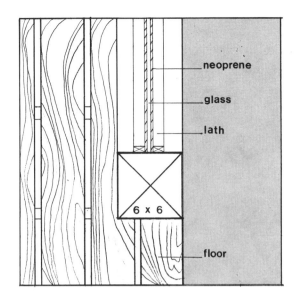

3

4

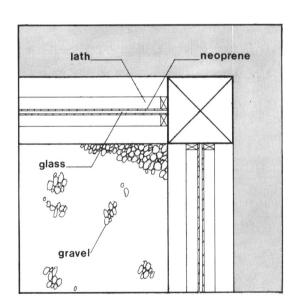

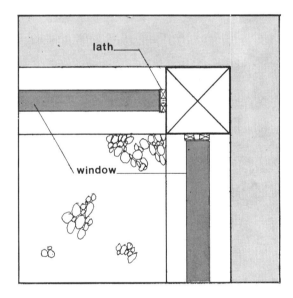

5

6

WINDOW DETAILS

Forrest Liles

Fig. 7

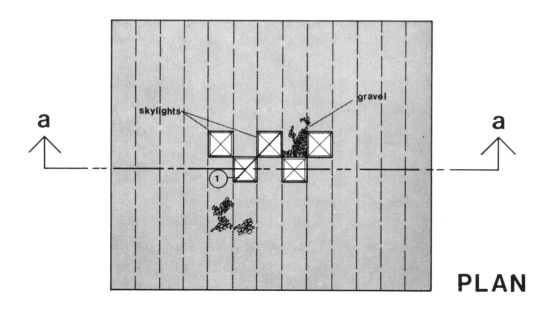

PLAN

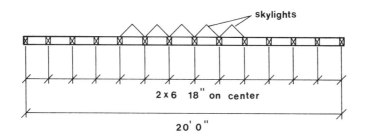

SECTION a-a

2 x 6 18" on center

20' 0"

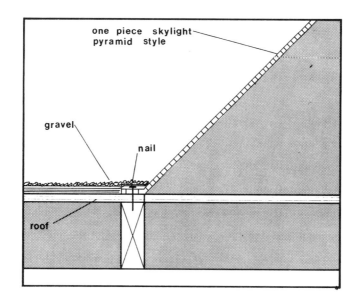

one piece skylight
pyramid style

gravel

nail

roof

DETAIL ①

PLASTIC SKYLIGHT
Forrest Liles

Fig. 8

INTERIOR VIEW

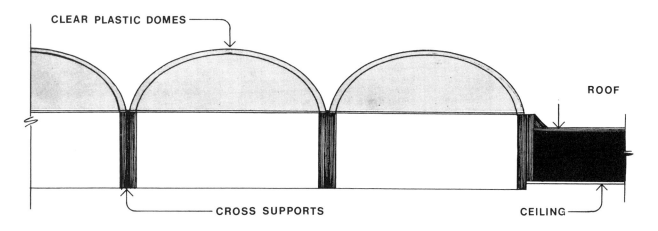

CLEAR PLASTIC DOMES

ROOF

CROSS SUPPORTS

CEILING

DETAIL

PLANTS UNDER SKYLIGHT   DESIGN: ADRIÁN MARTÍNEZ

Fig. 9

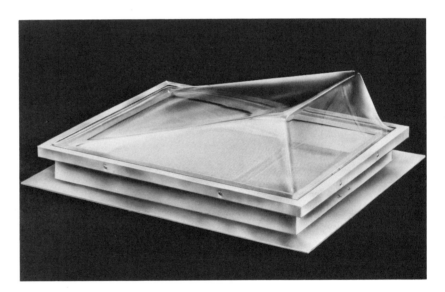

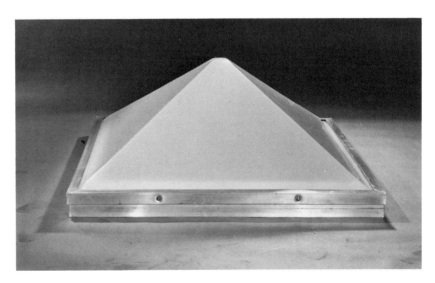

Commercial plastic domes for
garden room ceilings.
(Wascolite)

Double-stud next to doors and windows. When placing prefabricated units you may need a few shingles to square the units with the structure.

ROOFING

The roof is one of the more important parts of the garden room. There is an assortment of skylight and roofing materials, from plastic to glass, some quite elaborate, some very simple, and design is governed only by your imagination. One of the most unique ceiling constructions I have seen in some time uses movable shutters to direct the light in the garden room. Clerestory windows, flat-glass panels, peaked skylights, and domes of different shapes are all part of the exciting possibilities for roof designs. (See drawings 8, 9).

For glass inlaid in the roof, use preformed plastic tape to bed and cushion the glass. Generally, tempered or wire glass is necessary in ceilings (and required by building codes) although occasionally, as in clerestory window construction, double-strength window glass is allowed. (Check local codes first to be sure.)

Copper or galvanized flashing is necessary to eliminate the possibility of water seeping back inside the structure from the outside. Flashing is also required on any outside wood sheathing or wall facing if a butt joint is required.

Don't forget gutters to carry off excess rainwater, and be sure there are drainage facilities for roofing glass.

Recommended Accessories for Equipping a Garden Room

Automatic watering system
Water supply (hot and cold)
Work area
Plant benches and shelves
Soil storage
Sink
Humidifier
Shading
Electrical power (lights, outlets, etc.)
Automatic ventilators
Independent heating system
Hose bibbs

Construction Supplies

Nails 6-8-10
String
Carpenter's level
Steel rods (foundation)
Conduit and electrical outlet boxes
Conduit staples
Carpenter's square
Skill saw
Hammer
Shingles
Hand saw
Building materials (lumber, framing, mouldings)
Drain tiles
Several yards of sand and gravel to lay drain tiles

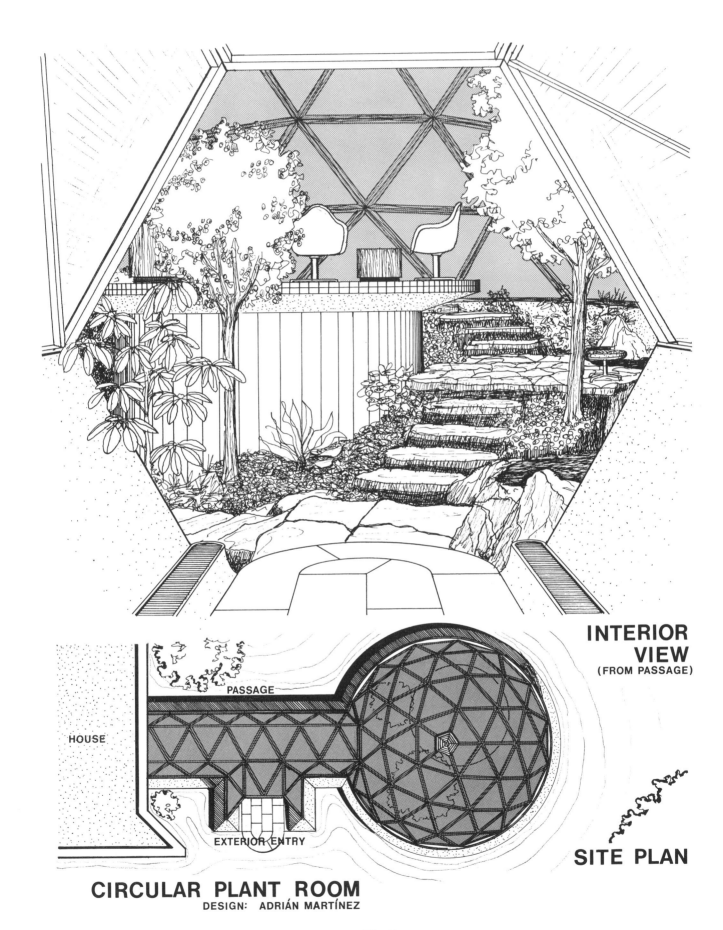

INTERIOR VIEW
(FROM PASSAGE)

PASSAGE

HOUSE

EXTERIOR ENTRY

SITE PLAN

CIRCULAR PLANT ROOM
DESIGN: ADRIÁN MARTÍNEZ

Fig. 10

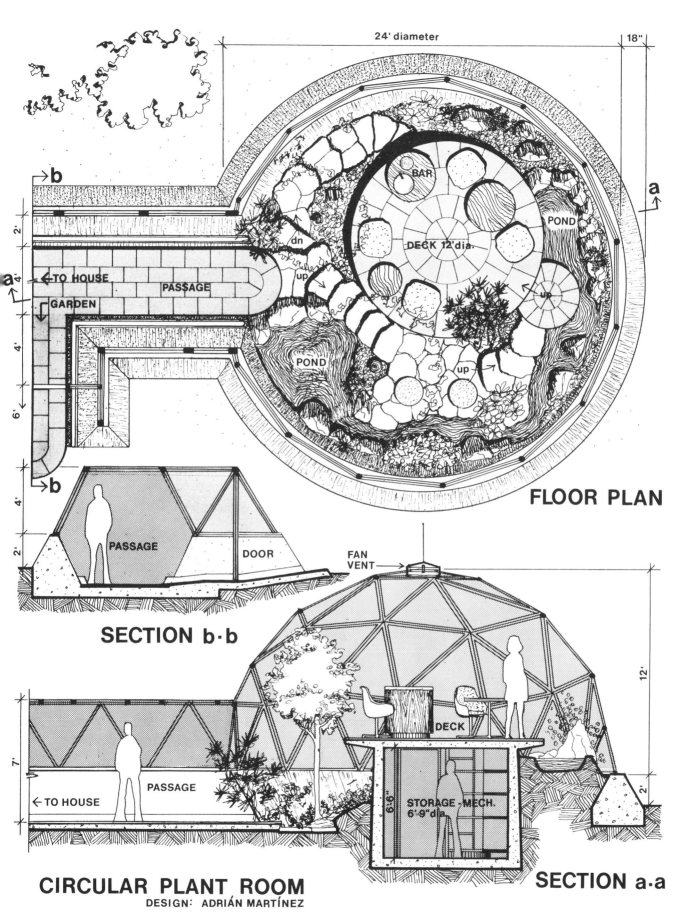

24' diameter

18"

b

a

2'

4'

4'

6'

4'

2'

← TO HOUSE

PASSAGE

GARDEN

dn

up

DECK 12' dia.

BAR

POND

POND

up

up

a

FLOOR PLAN

b

PASSAGE

DOOR

SECTION b·b

FAN VENT

DECK

12'

7'

← TO HOUSE

PASSAGE

STORAGE - MECH.
6' 9" dia.

9'·9"

2'

CIRCULAR PLANT ROOM
DESIGN: ADRIÁN MARTÍNEZ

SECTION a·a

Fig. 11

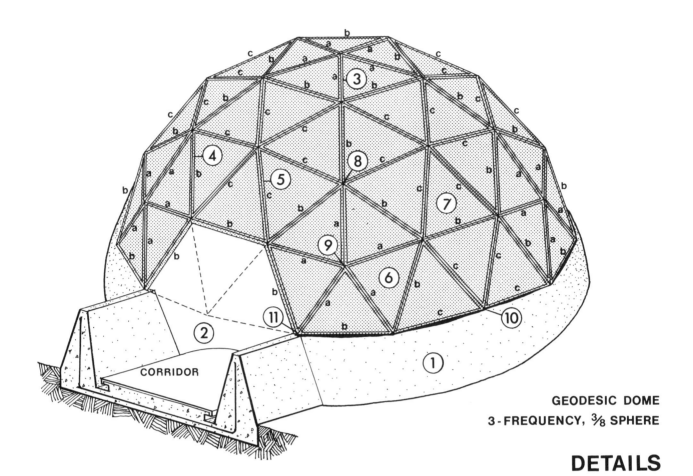

GEODESIC DOME
3 - FREQUENCY, ⅜ SPHERE

DETAILS

FOUNDATION WALL

① REINFORCED CONCRETE

FLOOR

② PAVED & LANDSCAPED

ROOF STRUCTURE

③ WOOD OR STEEL, 30- $50\frac{3}{16}$" 'a' STRUTS

④   "   "   40 - $58\frac{1}{8}$" 'b'   "

⑤   "   "   46 - $59\frac{3}{8}$" 'c'   "

ROOF INFILL

⑥ PLASTIC PANELS, 30 -'a·b·a' TRIANGLES

⑦   "   "   41 -'c·b·c'   "

JOINTS

⑧ 25 - 6 SPOKE HUBS

⑨ 6 - 5   "   "

⑩ 12 - 4   "   "

⑪ 2 - 3   "   "

NOTE: THIS IS ONLY AN OUTLINE GUIDE FOR THE EXTERIOR STRUCTURE

MATERIALS

CIRCULAR PLANT ROOM
DESIGN: ADRIÁN MARTÍNEZ

Fig. 12

INTERIOR VIEW

TWO-STORY GLASS GALLERY
DESIGN: ADRIÁN MARTÍNEZ

Fig. 13

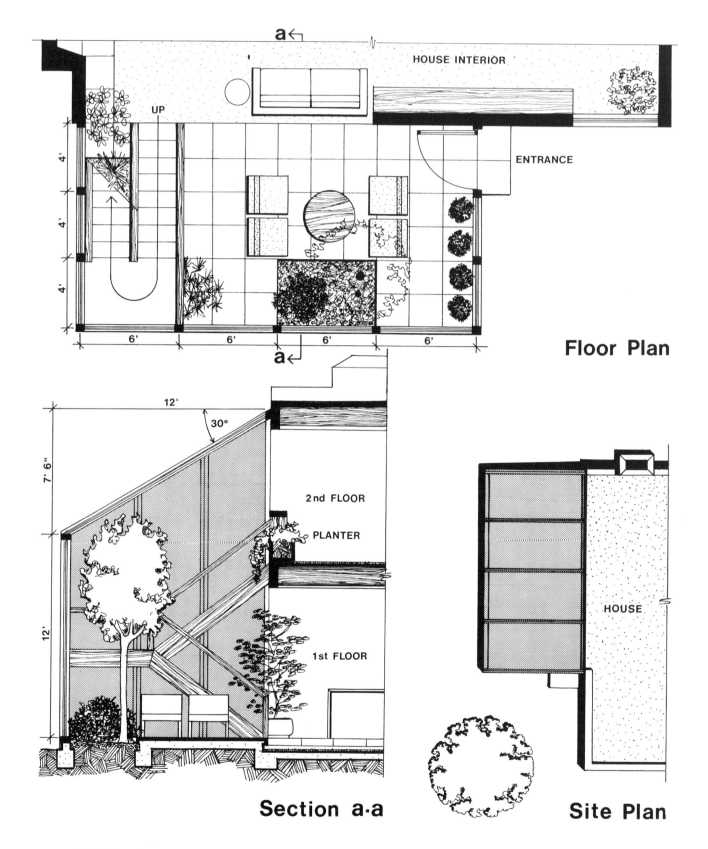

Floor Plan

HOUSE INTERIOR

UP

ENTRANCE

4' 4' 4'

6' 6' 6' 6'

a

12'

30°

7' 6"

2nd FLOOR

PLANTER

1st FLOOR

12'

Section a·a

HOUSE

Site Plan

TWO-STORY GLASS GALLERY
DESIGN: ADRIÁN MARTÍNEZ

Fig. 14

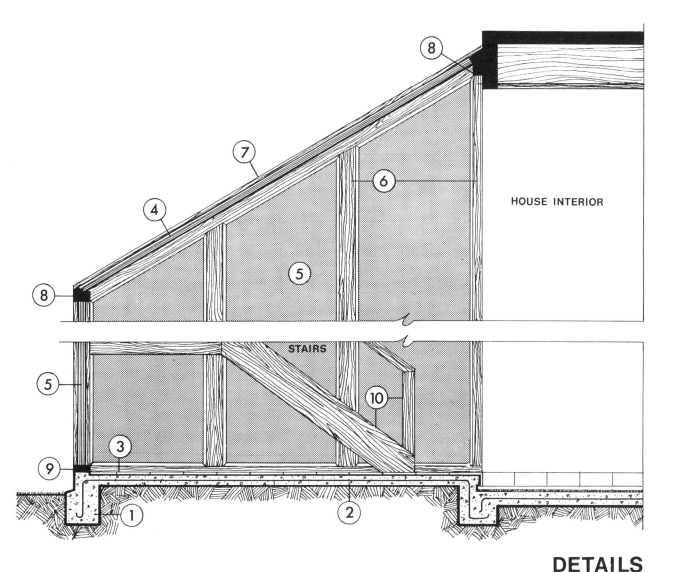

HOUSE INTERIOR

STAIRS

DETAILS

FOUNDATIONS

① REINFORCED CONCRETE

FLOOR

② CONCRETE

③ QUARRY TILE 212 SQ. FT.

ROOF

④ WIRE GLASS, METAL FRAMED

WINDOW WALLS

⑤ GLASS, METAL FRAMED & GLASS DOOR

STRUCTURE

⑥ POSTS 6 x 6's, 5- 12', 2 - 15', 2 - 17', 3 x 6's, 2 -19'

⑦ BEAMS 5 - 6 x 8's x 15'

⑧ PLATE 8 - 4 x 6's x 6'

⑨ SILL 2 x 6's, 1 - 24', 1 -12', 1-8'

STAIR

⑩ LAMINATED WOOD

NOTE: THIS GARDEN ROOM IS PART OF THE HOUSE

MATERIALS

TWO-STORY GLASS GALLERY
DESIGN: ADRIÁN MARTÍNEZ

Fig. 15

INTERIOR VIEW

NORTH

GARDEN

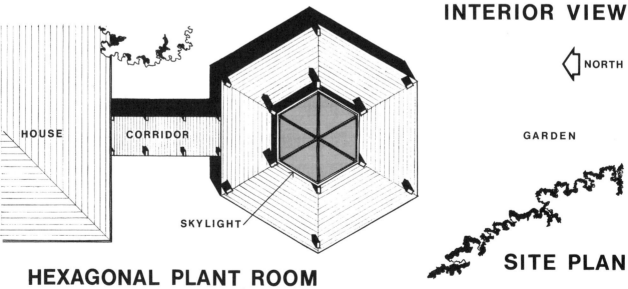

HEXAGONAL PLANT ROOM
DESIGN: ADRIÁN MARTÍNEZ

HOUSE · CORRIDOR · SKYLIGHT

SITE PLAN

Fig. 16

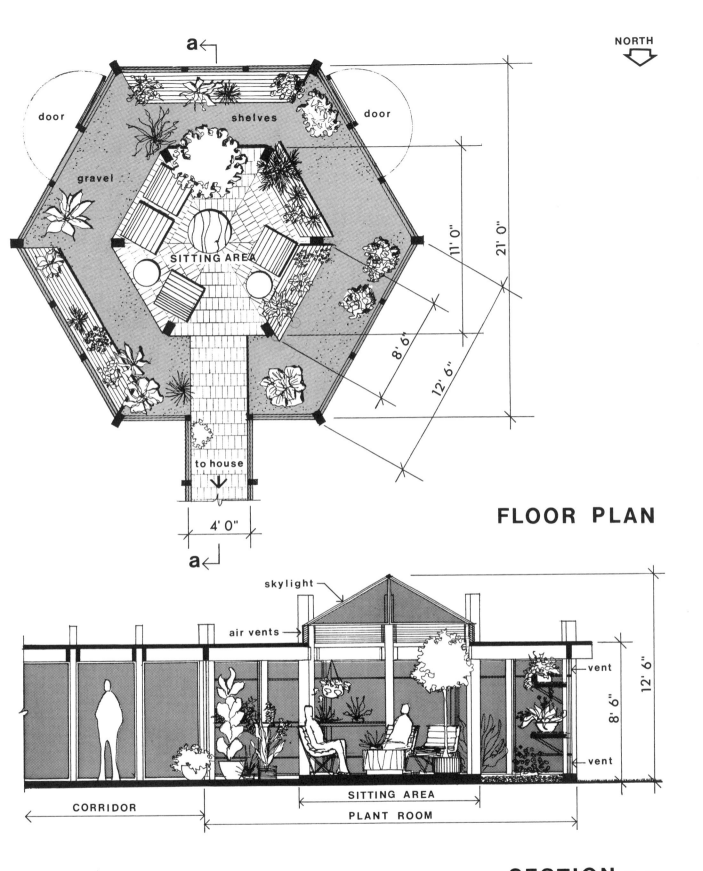

NORTH

a

door   shelves   door

gravel

SITTING AREA

to house

21' 0"

11' 0"

8' 6"

12' 6"

4' 0"

a

FLOOR PLAN

skylight

air vents

vent

12' 6"

8' 6"

vent

CORRIDOR

SITTING AREA

PLANT ROOM

SECTION a·a

HEXAGONAL PLANT ROOM
DESIGN: ADRIÁN MARTÍNEZ

Fig. 17

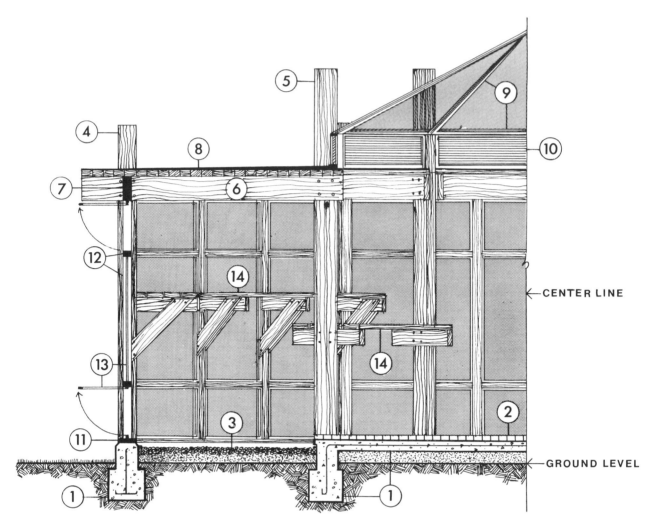

← CENTER LINE

← GROUND LEVEL

DETAILS

FOUNDATIONS

① REINFORCED CONCRETE *

FLOOR

② BRICK   130 SQ. FT. (over concrete)*
③ GRAVEL   40 CUBIC FT. (over sand)

STRUCTURE

④ OUTER POSTS 6 – 4 x 8's x 9' 6"
⑤ INNER POSTS 6 – 4 x 8's x 11'
* CORRIDOR POSTS   4 x 4's x 9' 6"
⑥ RADIAL BEAMS 12 – 2 x 10's x 8'
⑦ PERIMETER BEAMS 6 – 4 x 10's x 12'
* CORRIDOR BEAMS   2 x 10's x 5'

* corridor materials will depend upon its length

ROOF

⑧ PLANKS 2 x 6 TONGUE & GROOVE
BUILT-UP ROOFING 450 SQ. FT. *
⑨ TEMPERED OR WIRE GLASS, STEEL FRAMED
SKYLIGHT
⑩ LOUVERS   PAINTED ALUMINUM

WINDOW WALLS

⑪ SILLS 6 – 2 x 8's x 12' 6" *
⑫ FRAMING 1 x 2's & 2 x 4's *
⑬ GLASS FIXED & OPERABLE (aluminum frame)
                                                    *

PLANT SHELVES

⑭ SUPPORTS & PLANKS 2 x 6's

MATERIALS

HEXAGONAL PLANT ROOM
DESIGN: ADRIÁN MARTÍNEZ

Fig. 18

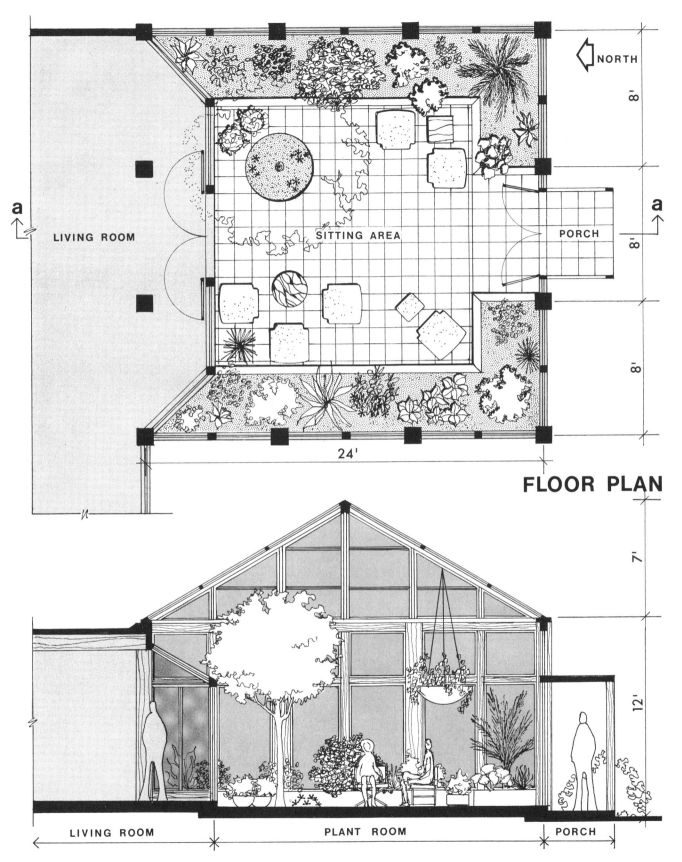

NORTH

8'

8'

8'

LIVING ROOM

SITTING AREA

PORCH

24'

FLOOR PLAN

7'

12'

LIVING ROOM

PLANT ROOM

PORCH

SECTION a·a

SQUARE PLANT ROOM
DESIGN: ADRIÁN MARTÍNEZ

Fig. 19

INTERIOR VIEW

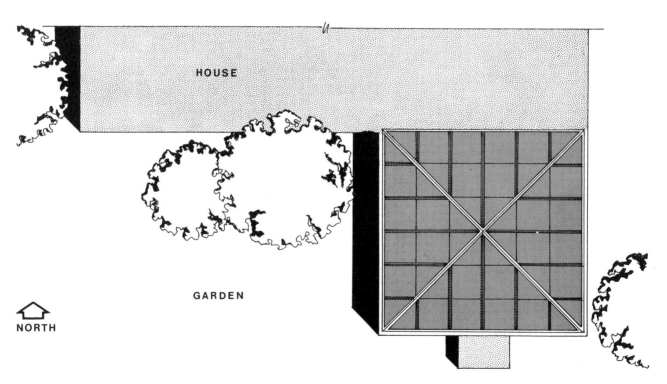

HOUSE

GARDEN

NORTH

SQUARE PLANT ROOM
DESIGN: ADRIÁN MARTÍNEZ

SITE PLAN

Fig. 20

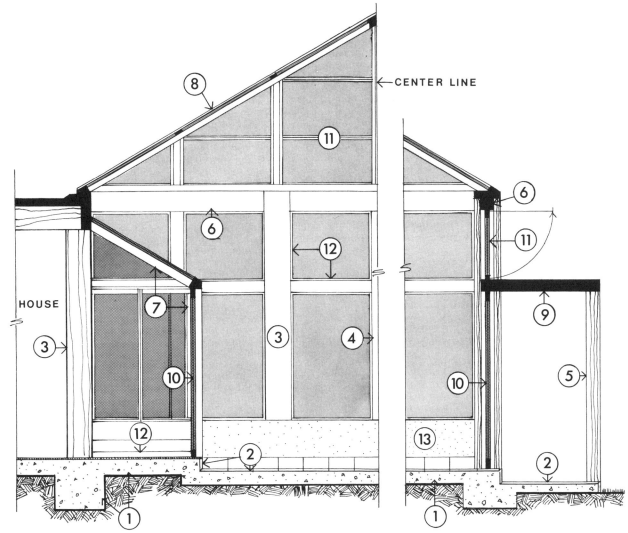

CENTER LINE

HOUSE

DETAILS

FOUNDATIONS–FLOOR

① REINFORCED CONCRETE
② QUARRY TILE 275 SQ. FT.

STRUCTURE

③ MAIN POSTS 12 - 12 x 12's x 12'
④ INTERMEDIATE POSTS 8 - 6 x 6's x 12'
⑤ PORCH POSTS 2 - 3 x 6's x 7' 6"
⑥ PERIMETER BEAMS 12 - 6 x 8's x 7'
⑦ BAY WINDOW 6 x 6's, 2 x 6's

ROOF/SKYLIGHT

⑧ STEEL FRAMED SKYLIGHT, WIRE GLASS
⑨ PORCH 2 x 6 s x 4' 6"

WINDOW WALLS

⑩ STEEL FRAMED GLASS DOORS
⑪ GLASS, FIXED & OPERABLE
⑫ SILLS & FRAMING 2 x 2's, 2 x 6's

PLANT BEDS

⑬ REINFORCED CONCRETE

MATERIALS

SQUARE PLANT ROOM
DESIGN: ADRIÁN MARTÍNEZ

Fig. 21

Plant Room Interior View

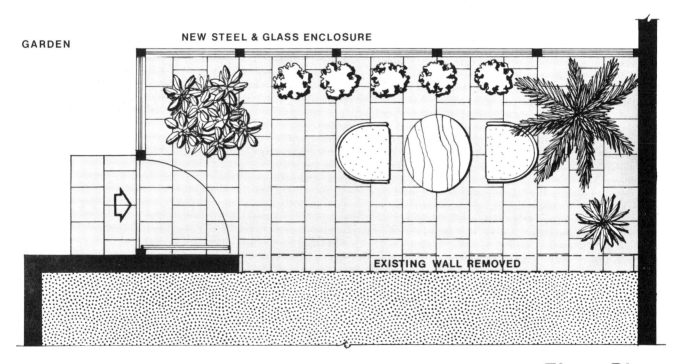

Floor Plan

OPENING a ROOM   DESIGN: ADRIÁN MARTÍNEZ

Fig. 22

The author's garden room showing the outdoor garden area.
(Joyce R. Wilson)

Louvered shutters in the ceiling are a feature of this garden room; they afford ideal light situations for plants.
(Max Eckert photo; La Chance, Interior Designer)

Strong architectural lines are provided by redwood and glass allowing for a small reflecting pool and adequate growing conditions for a carpet of grass. The ceiling is screen wire, floor, painted concrete bordered in brick.
(Hedrich-Blessing photo; William R. Jenkins, Architect)

A lovely place to relax is this color-filled garden room; bougainvillea and orchids grow with ferns and bromeliads. The floor is brick, ceiling glass.
(Joyce R. Wilson photo; Andrew R. Addkison, Interior Designer)

Plant Room Interior View

Floor Plan

STEPS

NEW SKYLIGHT

EXISTING STRUCTURE

GLASS ENCLOSURE

NEW TILE FLOOR

HOUSE INTERIOR

CONVERTING a PORCH   DESIGN: ADRIÁN MARTÍNEZ

Fig. 23

An old-fashioned picket-fenced concrete porch adjacent to the living room was the site of the author's garden room (left). The site for the new garden room is being readied; the foundation has been poured to extend the existing porch, the brick work is being installed (middle). The framing for the walls is set in place; French doors replace the existing wall of the living room (bottom).
(Jack Kramer)

Butterfly roof detail, as the garden room takes shape. *(Jack Kramer)*

The completed garden room. *(Morley Baer)*

This small solarium is used for growing orchids;
the casement windows and tile floor add to the
charm of the room.
(Jack Kramer)

CHAPTER 3

Atriums and Solariums (Sun Porches)

The word *atrium* originally designated the central room of a Roman house or an open court. Its function was as a reception court rather than as a place for plants. Today's atrium generally is the center area of a contemporary home, with rooms opening onto a vista of sky and greenery. Although the atrium is a place for plants, it also provides good air circulation and light within the house. This dual-functioning area is being incorporated more and more into contemporary homes, since open land is at a premium and the atrium provides a garden in the home.

A solarium is generally located on an upper floor of a house—although it need not be—and is specifically a place for plants. It is usually a room with a complete glass roof; though while today solariums may not have full glass ceilings, essentially the sides are enclosed in glass.

The atrium and the solarium are different in design and construction, but each has something to offer the indoor gardener, and each is an area to bring outdoors indoors. The solarium can be added to an existing structure; the atrium is almost always incorporated into the design of the home. Yet each offers the owner a chance to have living green plants within the home when outdoor space is limited.

GARDENS IN THE HOME

The atrium, surrounded as it is by the walls or windows of the house, has many advantages, and is becoming as popular in the East as it is in California and Florida. It is a perfect solution to city gardens, offers complete privacy, gives light and color within the house, and roofed over makes a spectacular conservatory. The trick of a successful atrium is to make it large enough so air can circulate in it and sun can reach it several hours a day rather than only at noon.

Because this garden area occupies the center of the house, it is always on display, so choose plants for it with a keen eye. Planning this room, which is generally square or rectangular, requires good design, for it means working in a confined space. There must be room both for plants and for people to stroll.

For a successful atrium, vary the window or wall decor by using trellises, lathing, or some design element to carry the eye around the area. Use planting pockets within the room for graceful greenery, and select a sophisticated flooring, such as hand-hewn tile or quarry. Choose plants as though they were pieces of furniture, for indeed they are the furnishings of the room. This is the area where you want lovely standards—roses and fuchsias in ornamental containers and stately topiaries—and dramatic specimen plants. Rather than planting in the ground, use ornamental containers to show off the plants. For a tropical effect use palms against the window walls, or vines as tracery to add pattern. Select plants with an eye for vertical and horizontal accents; this is not the place for bushy, unkempt specimens but rather well-trimmed and handsome plants. Balance small-leaved foliage with large-leaved plants and strive for harmony within the atrium—a repetition of

Inside the atrium one feels the forest; the soaring ceiling
becomes the sky.
(Guy Burgess photo; Hobart Wagener, Architect)

This elegant atrium has a unique ceiling structure; the plants are mainly in the ground, forming a lush frame visible from all rooms of the home.

(Guy Burgess photo; Hobart Wagener, Architect)

Close-up of interior planting in the atrium.

(Guy Burgess photo; Hobart Wagener, Architect)

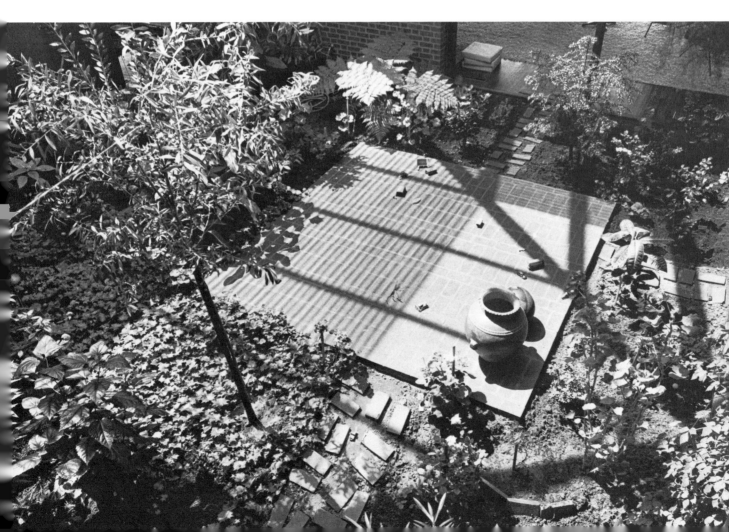

pattern, materials, and so forth. And you can use a small statue, lantern, or piece of sculpture to accent the room.

A suitable glass roof, skylights, or domes should be considered (see Chapter 2); an open atrium will limit plant selection and, in hot climates, the room to only occasional use.

Although the atrium should have ample planting to make it look like a garden, do not crowd the room so much that it becomes a jungle. Remember that you will cross this area to get to other rooms in the house, and that the prospect of late evening strolls under the stars will tempt your guests into the atrium. Leave enough space so people can meander through the indoor garden.

SOLARIUMS FOR EXOTICS

If you love plants and are prepared to devote a room to them, the solarium is your answer to an indoor garden. This glassed-in area is suitable for all kinds of plants, from orchids to azaleas, but don't be fooled into thinking that this lovely garden will grow on its own. A good part of your time will have to be devoted to the care of plants, for, like a greenhouse, the solarium is primarily a place for plants, and special conditions exist.

If you select the solarium as your garden, be sure to provide sufficient air circulation within the area. Have windows that will open easily to let in air, for ventilation is the secret of growing healthy plants in this atmosphere. Maintaining a humid atmosphere is also a necessity, as is light; the solarium should be generally located on the south side of the house so it will be flooded with sun almost all day.

Be prepared to water plants almost every day and sometimes twice a day in the summer. Install plant shelves and benches; avoid putting pots directly on the floor because this encourages hiding places for insects. Place your plants at different levels for eye interest, and don't forget to have hanging baskets.

Although the atrium and garden room may not provide enough sun for all flowering plants, the solarium, on the other hand, will suit almost any flowering exotic. This room should be a mass of bright color and cheer; it should not present an understated picture like the atrium or a casual greenery like the garden room.

Here are some general rules for growing plants in the solarium:

Provide adequate ventilation at all times, even in winter. Water plants copiously, every day in summer, about four times a week in winter.

Inspect plants frequently for signs of disease or pests. Repot plants yearly for maximum growth; in solarium conditions, plants use up soil nutrients quickly.

Provide a drop in temperature and humidity at night; ideal conditions would be 85 to 90 degrees F. during the day and 65 to 70 degrees F. at night.

Plants for Atriums

Aechmea fasciata
Agave americana marginata (century plant)
Aloe arborescens
Araucaria excelsa (Norfolk Island pine)
Aspidistra elatior (cast-iron plant)
Asplenium nidus (bird's nest fern)
Bambusa (bamboo)
Camellia sasanqua
Chamaedorea erumpens (bamboo palm)
Chlorophytum elatum (spider plant)
Cissus rhombifolia (grape ivy)
Citrus (lemon, orange, lime)
Clerodendron thompsoniae (bleeding heart glorybower)
Dizygotheca elegantissima
Epiphyllum hybrids (orchid cactus)
Ficus benjamina (weeping fig)
Ficus lyrata (fiddle-leaf fig)
Guzmania lingulata
Monstera deliciosa (Swiss cheese plant)
Nephrolepis exaltata (Boston fern varieties)
Nerium oleander (oleander)
Plumbago capensis (Cape plumbago)
Polypodium aureum
Rhapis excelsa (lady palm)
Schefflera actinophylla (Australian umbrella tree)

Plants for Solariums

Abutilon hybridum
Aechmea chantini
Allamanda cathartica
Anthurium scherzerianum (flamingo flower)
Billbergia venezuelana
Bougainvillea
Columnea hybrids
Dendrobium pierardi

Dipladenia amoena
Epidendrum o'brienianum
Episcia hybrids
Gardenia jasminoides
Hedychium coronarium (white ginger lily)
H. gardnerianum (kahili ginger lily)
Heliconia angustifolia
H. aurantiaca
Hibiscus rosa-sinensis (Chinese hibiscus)

Hylocereus hybrids (night-blooming cactus)
Medinilla magnifica (love plant)
Pelargoniums (geraniums)
Rhipsalis paradoxa (chain cactus)
Rhyncostylis gigantea
Schlumbergera bridgesi (Christmas cactus)
Sobralia macrantha
Vanda hybrids

Tropical plants abound in this small atrium, the
focal point of the home. The plants are alocasia and
philodendron, in the background; the center plant is
a fine cycad.
(Hort-Pix)

CHAPTER 4

The Indoor Pool Greenery

New materials and new methods of construction today make the indoor pool a reality instead of a dream, and this enclosed area provides year-round greenery as well as a place to swim. Wire mesh, plastic, and glass are the necessary ceiling materials; generally follow garden room ceiling and wall construction (see Chapter 2).

Like the outdoor swimming pool, the enclosed pool must be landscaped to be handsome. A bare expanse of water is rarely pleasing without some green plants to show it off, and, in a pool situation where there is an abundance of natural light, plants thrive. Any plant that will grow in a garden room (see Chapter 5) will do well in a pool situation.

PLANTS AT POOLSIDE

As a general rule the plants will be in containers, and there are dozens of species that can be planted in ornamental tubs and boxes at poolside. What you choose depends, naturally, on your budget, but usually large specimen plants and seasonal pot plants are needed to add color to the scene. Tropical plants are the best selections, since the enclosed swimming pool is warm and quite humid. Ferns and palms will thrive; so will orchids.

Easy-to-grow plants are the answer to poolside gardening, since basically the pool area offers little space. The plants are for decoration and to guide traffic; they serve as accessories in the room rather than as the feature, as in garden rooms.

PLACING PLANTS

An isolated plant next to the pool is hardly attractive, but a group of plants in an island pattern makes a fine highlight. As in outdoor landscaping, large plants should be placed in the rear and smaller ones near the pool edge. Use plants to guide traffic around the pool, as vertical accents near doorways and windows, and for mass and volume along pool sides (but far enough from the edge so as not to interfere with traffic).

Since most pool areas are large (the average pool is 15′ by 30′), small trees in tubs are effective in corners, and large palms are always appealing. You want a lush natural feeling to complement the pool area; in many ways the greenery should act as a frame for the pool, the water being a perfect foil for the silhouettes of leaves.

High ceilings are a natural part of pool enclosures, so hanging plants in suitable containers are especially attractive. They can be fully appreciated, at eye level, and will furnish a needed vertical accent. (Among the many plants for basket growing are ferns and gesnerads, orchids, geraniums, and begonias.) Place such plants high enough so they will not interfere with traffic but low enough to reach for watering. Use two or three pots in tandem (one below the other) for a stunning effect.

CARE OF PLANTS

Large-container plants require suitable care if they are to prosper: feeding and watering, potting and repotting. These plants are costly and at the peak of perfection and with reasonable care they can decorate the area for many years. Most plants do not need full sunlight, but ample bright light is necessary for healthy growth.

Place the containers where you want them before you plant them, because large tubs and boxes filled with soil are heavy to move, even on dollies. Water pool plants thoroughly and deeply and then let them dry out before rewatering. If possible, soak the plants once a month in a tub of water for several hours, or until the water stops bubbling. This type of watering leaches out built-up salts that can harm plants and keep the root ball from drawing away from the container walls, thus causing a well. Remember that, if soil is allowed to get caked, the root ball shrinks, and the water will run down the sides of the pot rather than into the root network.

Do not allow soil to be constantly wet; it should merely be moist to the touch. Overwatering creates a soggy soil, so air cannot get through. When plants can't get air at the roots, they suffocate or drown.

Select plants from the list in Chapter 5.

INTERIOR VIEW

ENCLOSED SWIMMING POOL
DESIGN:ADRIÁN MARTÍNEZ

Fig. 24

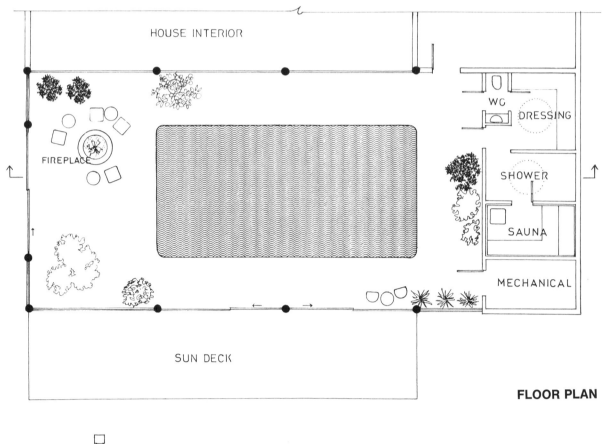

HOUSE INTERIOR

WC

DRESSING

FIREPLACE

SHOWER

SAUNA

MECHANICAL

SUN DECK

FLOOR PLAN

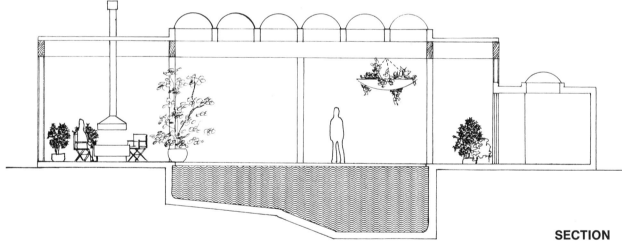

SECTION

ENCLOSED SWIMMING POOL
DESIGN:ADRÍAN MARTÍNEZ

Fig. 25

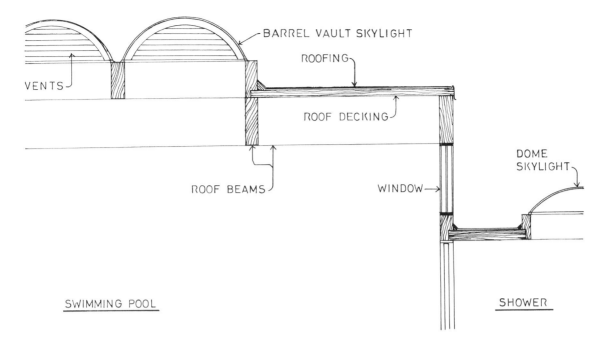

BARREL VAULT SKYLIGHT

ROOFING

VENTS

ROOF DECKING

ROOF BEAMS

WINDOW

DOME SKYLIGHT

SWIMMING POOL

SHOWER

DETAIL A-A

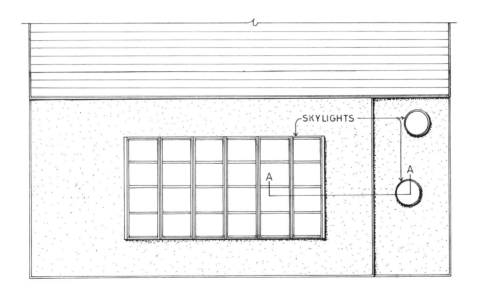

SKYLIGHTS

A

A

ROOF PLAN

ENCLOSED SWIMMING POOL
DESIGN: ADRIÁN MARTÍNEZ

Fig. 26

Plants of all kinds frame this pool-garden room. The
handsomely designed ceiling provides major eye interest.
*(Harr, Hedrich-Blessing photo; George Fred Keck &
William Keck, Architects)*

Open to the sky, this elegant atrium brimming
with colorful plants is a delight to the eye.
(Max Eckert photo; Joe Copp, Interior Designer)

This private pool is also a garden room; hanging plants grace the brick wall with seasonal potted plants for added color. The floor is varnished wood slats and the ceiling crowned with plastic domes...a totally inviting room.
(Hedrich-Blessing photo; Edward Dart, AIA Architect)

The planting island at the right is a perfect accent for this
pool; Cyperus, Aralia, and tropical banana plants are used.
At the entrance is a fine phoenix palm.
(Hedrich-Blessing photo; Robert Fitch Smith, Architect)

This pool relies on large houseplants to give it color and dimension; the skylights afford excellent light for plant growth. Plants are dracaenas and *Ficus lyrata*.
(Hedrich-Blessing photo; Alden Dow & Associates, Architects)

This handsome pool shows a unique ceiling structure;
outdoor plants combine with indoor plantings to establish
a harmonious and lovely area.
(Hedrich-Blessing photo; Martin Bros., Builders)

This indoor pool has its own lovely planting area at the
right; without the greenery the pool would seem sterile.
(Hedrich-Blessing photo; Coder Taylor & Associates, Architects)

Lush plantings frame an indoor pool; note the geometrical lines
of the pool for eye interest; they act as planting islands.
The ceiling is glass in aluminum frames. An ideal room.

(Max Eckert)

Philodendrons, begonias, ferns, and bromeliads create a
lush picture in this tropical garden room.

(Hort-Pix)

CHAPTER 5

Garden Room Plants

The world of indoor plants is far different from what it was even a few years ago. Sophisticated heating and humidity systems are now standard installations in most new construction, and, because of controlled temperature and humidity, many plants that thrived only in conservatories can be now grown indoors. Also, a host of new plants is available from plant suppliers, and more species appear yearly.

Large tubbed trees and shrubs indoors are no longer uncommon; indeed, these plants are needed for properly furnishing a garden room. Philodendrons and dieffenbachias are still with us, but such unusual exotic plants as *Ficus benjamina* (a charming lacy tree) and graceful cycads and palms are taking their place indoors and thriving.

For garden room growing, use large foliage plants such as *Pandanus veitchii* and *Araucaria excelsa* and dramatic succulents like *Agave americana* and yucca. Flowering gems from the Orchid and Bromeliad families and wonderful epiphyllums also add color to the special room.

SPECIMEN TREES AND SHRUBS

A specimen plant is mature, large, and at its peak of beauty. It can be 8 to 15 feet tall, a tree or a shrub, a succulent or cactus, an orchid or bromeliad. It can be graceful or bold in appearance. It will cost as much as a piece of furniture, and if cared for properly will last as long. Some plants are massive and branching, others bold and dramatic, and still others delicate and fragile; a plant's form may be columnar, pyramidal, globe-like, open, or dense, and there are all kinds of plants for all kinds of situations.

Many times all that is needed in the garden room is one stellar specimen used as a feature; other times you may want a group of plants along a wall to guide eye interest. The plants you use depend upon the room's size, shape, and attitude, as well as upon available light, maintenance, color and texture of leaves, and form and resistance to insects and disease.

At one time it was difficult to locate large plants and impossible to have them shipped and arrive in good condition. Now several suppliers in large cities (the Greenhouse and Terrestris in New York and Chicago, for examples) stock specimen plants, as do some mail-order suppliers and local retail nurseries. Plants can be purchased or rented.

Air freight brings plants to you overnight from almost any place in the United States. Just last week I received some 9-foot orchids in perfect condition; they made the journey in sixteen hours from Chicago to my doorstep in California.

Although there are many plants that will thrive indoors indefinitely, some do better than others. The Ficus family includes many small trees with graceful branches and finely toothed leaves. Camellias offer many attractive flowering varieties, some of which grow to ceiling height. Large succulents are nature's sculpture, and can be used effectively in many interiors, and hibiscus and bromeliads, orchids and ferns, palms and dwarf fruit trees are all possibilities for the unique room.

The following large plants have been chosen because they perform well indoors and have outstanding characteristics.

Plant Lists

Plant	Description	Shape	Remarks
Acanthus mollis (Grecian urn plant)	Large deep-green, lobed leaves; rigid flower spike	Rosette	Vertical accent
Aeonium arboreum	A handsome rosette of lush leaves to 3 feet	Rosette	For mass and horizontal accent; grows well in same pot for years
Agave americana variegata	Dark-green and yellow leaves, highly sculptured; can grow to 5 feet across	Rosette	A dramatic display
A. attenuata	Gray-green foliage; twisted growth	Rosette	Fine specimen plant; needs little care
Araucaria excelsa	Needlelike, glossy green leaves	Pyramidal	As sculptural feature
Aucuba japonica	Polished dark-green foliage	Dense leaves, round shape	For room corners
Begonia (angel wing)	Lush apple-green foliage; colorful pendant blooms	Generally a cascading plant	For color in hanging containers
Begonia (rhizomatous)	Large plants and varied kinds	Upright or trailing	Tough plants that can take abuse
Beloperone guttata (shrimp plant)	Small dark-green leaves; colorful bracts	Sprawling	Old favorite
Camellia japonica	Dark-green leathery leaves; large flowers	Irregular shape	Needs coolness at night
C. sansanqua	Dark-green leathery leaves; small flowers	Irregular shape	Needs coolness at night
Caryota mitis (fishtail palm)	Wedge-shaped dark-green fronds	Branching	Highly decorative
Chamaedorea erumpens (bamboo palm)	Erect canes with leaflets	Very vertical	Good in room corners; a stalwart grower
Chlorophytum elatum (spider plant)	A graceful plant with green, arching leaves	A trailer when mature	Use on plant pedestals or in baskets
Cissus antarctica (kangaroo treebine)	Scalloped dark-green leaves	Upright or trailing	A good plant for shady places
Citrus (lemon, lime, orange)	Leathery, oval leaves; white blooms	Sculptural branching growth	Good floor plants for accent; need lots of water
Clerodendron thompsoniae (bleeding heart glory-bower)	Bright-green, large-leaved plant with stunning flowers	Low and round; dense	Accent plant for color
Clivia miniata (kaffir lily)	Straplike dark-green leaves and orange blossoms	Low and lush	Reliable bloomer; keep potbound
Coleus blumei	Many leaf colors	Dense and bushy	Highly decorative when mature
Crassula argentea (jade plant)	Small leathery leaves	Branching, full plant	Unusual and easy to grow
Cycas revoluta (sago palm)	Narrow dark-green leaf segments	Vertical, delicate	Tough palm with good lines
Cymbidium devonianum	Grasslike foliage; delightful blooms	Upright, with pendant flower spikes	A touch of the exotic
Dieffenbachia amoena	Broad dark-green leaves worked with narrow white stripes	Can grow to 6 feet	Good color; easy to grow
Dion purpusii	Dark green leaflets	Arching and spreading	Excellent accent plant
Dizygotheca elegantissima (threadleaf false aralia)	Dark, shiny green, and toothed leaflets	Graceful and arching	A temperamental plant; grow it somewhat dry
Dracaena marginata	Spear-shaped dark-green leaves	Branching, sculptural	A dramatic room accent against bare wall
D. fragrans 'massangeana' (corn plant)	Tufts of apple-green leaves	Treelike when mature	Excellent vertical accent
Echeveria 'Gypsy'	Fine light-gray, green scalloped leaves, edged rose	Bold and massive	Looks like carved jade; stunning
Epiphyllum varieties (crested cactus)	Scandent dark-green foliage; large, colorful flowers	Pendant	Hardly attractive out of bloom; splendid with flowers

Plant	Description	Shape	Remarks
Euphorbia splendens (crown of thorns)	Buttonlike dark green leaves; scarlet-red flowers	Branching and gnarled	Good pot plant
Ficus benjamina (weeping fig)	Leathery poplarlike leaves	Branching, graceful	Handsome tree
Grevillea robusta (silk oak)	Dark green fronds	Irregular shape	Different
Hedychium coronarium (white ginger lily)	Leafy plant with white flowers	Upright	Tough to bloom; needs heat and sun
Heliconia angustifolia	Similar to bird of paradise	Upright, to 3 feet	Unusual; good house plant
Hibiscus	Large bright-green leaves; huge flowers	Can grow to 5 feet; branching	A stunner in bloom and easy to grow; needs lots of water
Howea fosteriana	Dark-green fronds	Drooping leaflets	Indestructible palm
Hylocereus varieties	Broad cactus-type leaves; mammoth flowers	Pendant and graceful	An oddity but stunning
Laurus nobilis (sweet bay)	Long, dark-green, and leathery leaves	Compact, multistemmed tapering cone	Good in rows to guide traffic
Medinilla magnifica	Oval dark-green leaves; showy pink flowers	Angled and long stems	Brilliant flowering plant; use mature ones
Monstera deliciosa (Swiss cheese plant)	Mammoth, deeply scalloped leaves	Massive, sculptural	Always a good corner plant
Musa nana (dwarf banana)	Large dark-green leaves	Upright	An oddity but nice
Nephrolepis exaltata 'Bostoniensis' (Boston fern; many varieties)	Cascading green fronds	Handsome rosettes	Splendid in baskets
Nerium oleander	Dark-green leathery leaves; colorful flowers	Branching, spreading	Impossible to kill
Pandanus veitchii	Shiny green and white toothed leaves	Rosette; can grow to 6 feet in diameter	An overlooked fine display plant
Philodendron selloum	Deeply cut leaves	Branching, graceful	Makes nice accent
Phyllostachys (bamboo)	Grassy, needlelike leaves	Vertical, airy	Prettier than you think and easy to grow
Picea glauca 'Conica' (dwarf white spruce)	Fine, soft, and bright-green needles	Compact, pyramidal	Where mass is needed
Polypodium aureum (hare's foot fern)	Large bright-green fronds	Pendant	Excellent fern
Rhapis excelsa (lady palm)	Dark-green fronds	Fan shape	Vertical accent
Schefflera acontifolia	Dark-green leaves; frond growth	Canopy shape	Dramatic corner feature
Strelitzia reginae (bird-of-paradise)	Dark-green leaves; striking orange flowers	Upright, to 5 feet	Nice for bloom; needs wet soil
Syagrus weddellianum (coconut palm)	Feather-leaved palm	Central trunk	Decorative; grows slowly
Vallota speciosa (Scarborough lily)	Bulbous plant with strap-shaped evergreen leaves; clusters of bright orange-red flowers	Tall, to 4 feet	Excellent pot plant
Yucca aliofolia (Spanish bayonet)	Sharp, pointed leaves; dark green	Sculptural rosette	An overlooked plant that does well indoors

A small reflecting pool adds charm to an area; a large fern
accents the room.
(Hedrich-Blessing photo; George Fred Keck & William Keck, Architects)

OTHER GARDEN ROOM PLANTS

In addition to the plants listed, some plant groups offer species so decorative and lovely they deserve special mention. These include ferns and palms, cycads and dracaenas and epiphyllum (orchid cactus), ideal subjects for garden rooms.

Orchids, too, are not to be neglected when searching for dramatic, colorful blooms, and are covered in the next chapter.

Ferns

The ferns, as a group, offer a dazzling array of foliage accent. There are ferns with lacy fronds, while the fronds of others are wild and bold. Some are delicate, and many are fragile in appearance. In nature, ferns grow in moist, cool, and shady locations. In the house, they are handsome on pedestals or in plant stands at north or west exposures.

The selection of ferns is bewildering; one mail-order house lists over forty different ones. Although the Boston fern is perhaps the most popular, ferns like rabbit's foot and bird's nest are just too good to miss.

Place ferns in filtered light and give them a very porous soil of equal parts loam, leaf mold, and sand. Keep them moist but never soggy. I do not feed ferns; many times fertilizer burns leaf tips, and plants grow better without additional feeding.

Ferns should rest in winter, so decrease moisture and keep the soil barely damp. The plants prefer to be grown in small pots and disturbed as seldom as possible. If it is possible, put the pots on pebbles in trays so adequate moisture is provided—50 percent humidity is ideal.

Try the following ferns for beautiful foliage:

Adiantum cueatum. Old favorite. Dark-green fronds; many varieties including *A. c.* 'Excelsum,' 'Goldelse,' 'Matador'—all good, tolerant of adverse conditions.
A. hispidulum. Dwarf maidenhair fern; charming.
A. tenerum wrightii. Typical maidenhair; one of the best.
Asplenium nidus (bird's nest fern). Evergreen fronds. Outstanding.
A. viviparum. Very lacy fronds; produces plantlets on leaves.

Blechnum brasiliense. Coarse fronds. Low growing; different.
Davallia fejeensis (rabbit's foot fern). Fine feathery foliage and hairy, creeping rootstalks. A curiosity.
Nephrolepis exalata 'Bostoniensis' (Boston fern). Long pendant fronds. Easy to grow; robust.
N. e. 'Verona.' Lacy in appearance; compact growth.
Phyllitis scolopendrium. Pale-green, wide fronds.
Platycerium bifurcatum (common staghorn fern). Drooping fronds; grow in rafts of osmunda.
P. pumila. Upright fronds in fan shape; grow in rafts of osmunda.
Polypodium polycarpon. Strap-leaf fern, best grown on slab of osmunda.
Pteris ensiformis 'Victoriae.' Many forms; this one silver and green.
Woodwardia orientalis (chain fern). Excellent for basket growing.

Palms

We all know palms, and envision them as large trees growing in California and Florida. We rarely think of them as indoor plants, and yet many are superlative decorations that require little care. There are two kinds: those with feathery foliage and those with fan-shaped leaves.

Palms grow best in a soil mixture of equal parts of peat moss, loam, and sand. Put the plants where they receive bright light rather than sun, and keep the soil evenly moist all year except in winter—then keep them just barely moist. Most palms make their growth in spring and summer. Mist the foliage frequently to provide ample humidity in the air, and sponge the leaves with a damp cloth once a week.

Palms are at their best in large tubs; they grow for years in the same container and should not be repotted annually. A great many foliage plants require daily care, but palms, once adjusted to new conditions, need little care. They add charm and grace to any area.

Suggested palms:

Caryota (fishtail palm). Leaves wedge-shaped like a fishtail. Superlative house plant.
Chamaedorea Erumpens (bamboo palm). Most popular. Dwarf type, with graceful arching fronds.

Ferns, palms, and philodendrons offer dramatic color
for a garden room adjoining a bedroom. Plantings are
in the ground here, rather than in containers.
(Hort-Pix)

Chamaerops humilis. Never grows to more than 3 feet; has fan-shaped blue-green foliage. Likes a cool, airy spot.

Howea belmoreana. Very graceful. Single-trunked plant with long green leaves.

H. forsteriana. Pendant flat leaves from central stems; dark-green foliage. Grows quickly.

Livistona chinensis. Solitary trunk with large fan-shaped leaves. Needs space. Splendid corner accent.

Phoenix canariensis. Crowns of long, shiny, feathery green leaves; easily grown.

P. roebelenii (date palm). Dwarf variety with dark-green leaves. Outstanding as a pot plant.

Reinwardtia gracilis gracilior (window palm). Dwarf with windows in leaves. Unique.

Rhapis excelsa (lady palm). Indestructible, with green fan-shaped leaves.

R. humilis. Slightly smaller than *R. excelsa.*

Syagrus weddelliana. Dwarf with feathery yellow-green foliage. Graceful plant, but won't be with you for more than a few years.

Epiphyllums (Orchid Cactus)

This outstanding genus (native to Mexico, the West Indies, and Central and South America) is more commonly known as "orchid cactus." There are about twenty species prized for their large flowers, but it is the thousands of hybrids that steal the show. Crossed with Hylocereus and Selenicereus, epiphyllums produce flowers of incredible size and beauty. It would seem that such beauty would be difficult to cultivate, but epiphyllums are easy to grow. Most have scalloped, flat, and branchy growth, and the flowers are borne on the sides of the stems.

Remember that, although epiphyllums are cacti, they grow in tropical forests on trees. Basically, they are trailing plants, but they can be grown upright. Most epiphyllum species are large, awkward plants, and their beauty and popularity have prompted growers to develop more compact plants with flowers as attractive as their larger cousins. The hybrids come in almost every color and are incredibly free flowering. None grow more than 36 inches high, and many are about 24 inches.

Give these plants a porous soil mixture of one-half leaf mold with equal parts of coarse gravel and garden loam. Use small pots; the root system is scanty. Bright light and average home temperatures (72 degrees F. by day, 10 degrees less at night) suit most of the plants. Provide 30 to 50 percent humidity and allow the soil to dry out completely between waterings. Epiphyllum roots must not be surrounded by soggy soil. Repot the plants only when absolutely necessary; they resent any root disturbance. Do not feed the plants. Peak flowering is May and June. With careful selection, a dozen plants will give color in the garden room for about 2 months.

Try these for special beauty:

White, Cream, Yellow:
'Albino'
'Baby Doll'
'Champagne'
'Fanciful'
'Halo'
'Polar Bear'

Light Pink, Dark Pink:
'Angel Serenade'
'Fairy Queen'
'Flower Song'
'Princess Betty'
'Carnation'
'Cuthbert'

Orange:
'Cherokee Chief'
'Cup of Gold'
'Keepsake'
'Rosa Rita'
'Sunland'

Red:
'Bacchus'
'Cardinal'
'Fireside'
'Holiday'
'Imp'

Purple, Orchid:
'Adventure'
'Ceylon'
'Gertrude W. Beahm'
'Harmony'
'Jungle Night'

Cycads

Cycads are an ancient family of primitive plants from Africa and Australia. Generally, they resemble ferns, although crowns of leaves are borne from the trunks, similar to palm fronds. The foli-

Hanging baskets and seasonal potted plants are part of
a charming garden room.
(Max Eckert photo; Chris Christianson, Interior Designer)

Ferns blend beautifully with the total decor of this garden room.
Smaller seasonal plants are used as accents.
(Max Eckert photo; La Chance, Interior Designer)

Cut flowers show off this garden room; the curtains can
be drawn for weather protection.
(Max Eckert photo; Kathryn Crawford, Interior Designer)

A solarium can be the most colorful place in the home;
here Cinerarias and Hydrangeas are brilliant with color,
exquisite against a bank of house plants.
(Max Eckert photo; Kathryn Crawford Interior Designer)

Off the bedroom, a pleasant greenery is created in
little space and yet it is crowded with beautiful color:
chrysanthemums, geraniums, hydrangeas. The floor is random
slate and brown gravel; ceiling, wire screen.
(Hedrich-Blessing photo; Brooks Buderus, AIA, Architect)

age is leathery and smooth on the upper surface, with scales underneath. Most cycads are very slow growing, but their form and grace make them desirable.

Grow cycads in a basic potting soil and keep them warm, never less than 50 degrees F. at night. Give them bright light and keep the soil evenly moist, except in the winter, when they can be grown somewhat on the dry side. Mist the foliage frequently. Some good cycads to grow are:

Ceratozamia hilda. New; graceful dark-green leaves.
Cycas circinalis. Fern palms with shiny dark-green leaves.
C. revoluta (sago palm). Dark and shiny green leaves; ideal house plant.
Dion purpusii. Erect, stiff leaves with short trunk.
Macrozamia lucida. Small-growing leaves.
M. stenomera. Spiral fronds.
Zamia fischeri. Dwarf with dark-green leaves.

Dracaenas

Dracaenas, with their plain green foliage or variegated leaves, are found mainly on the west coast of Africa. The genus includes several plants that are extremely decorative. Some varieties tolerate shade, but the variegated kinds need some bright light. All survive a long time in average humidity, about 40 percent.

Because they come from an area where there is plentiful rainfall, the plants need a moisture-retentive soil of equal parts loam, peat moss, and sharp sand. Keep the medium moist but never soggy. Dracaenas should be repotted every year, as they do not thrive in the same container for too long.

Although there are many species, the following are especially good for accent in the garden room.

Dracaena deremensis 'Warneckii.' Gray and green leaves; good accent plant.
D. deremensis 'Longii.' Bright, striped green and white leaves on a central trunk.
D. fragrans 'Massangeana' (corn plant). Cream-colored stripes on broad leaves. Grows somewhat like a palm from a central core and becomes a handsome tree in a few years.
D. goddseffiana. Green leaves spattered with yellow; bushy growth, small size.
D. marginata. Handsome decorator plant with clusters of blade-shaped green leaves edged with red. Branches when young.
D. sanderiana. Gray-green, white-margined foliage. Especially good for dish gardens.

CARE OF PLANTS

Plants for garden rooms are apt to be costly, so you will want to keep them healthy and attractive to enjoy them as long as possible. Thus, proper care is necessary. This includes watering and feeding, potting and repotting, and prevention against insect attacks.

POTTING MIXES

The kind of soil you use for plants depends on your individual growing conditions and the plant. Choose soil that will hold moisture and yet allow drainage of excess water freely, since waterlogged soil quickly kills plants.

There are many, many potting mixes for plants. Nurseries have soil in sacks, garden centers have it in bulk, and some florists sell it by the bushel. I use a basic garden mix of 1 part garden loam, 1 part sand, and 1 part leaf mold. For cacti and succulents I add more sand, and for acid-loving azaleas and camellias I substitute 1 part peat moss for the leaf mold. Grow orchids and bromeliads in equal parts of shredded fir bark and osmunda or in fir bark alone.

Beware of no-soil mixes. These are referred to as peatlike mixes and evolved from several years research at Cornell University. Basically, they are composed of perlite or vermiculite and sphagnum peat moss. Sufficient nutrients must be added to them for plant growth. The mixes are lightweight —an advantage—but since the plants in them must be fed regularly, salts build up in the soil. This soil, without proper leaching, which is difficult to do with large containers, can harm plants quickly. Be prepared to devote more time to plants in soil-less mixes.

POTTING AND REPOTTING

Whatever growing medium you select, in time it will have to be renewed. Generally, plants in containers 16 inches or more can survive several

This garden area includes the glory-bower vine, Aglaonema,
and Spathiphyllum; the skylight provides ample light.
(Hort-Pix)

years without repotting; smaller containers need fresh soil more often. Do not set up a rigid schedule for repotting plants: observe your plants, and, when you see roots growing out of the bottom of the container or when the root ball has compacted and you see roots on the surface of the soil, repot the plant. Exceptions are clivias and some succulents and cacti that prefer to be potbound. For these, dig out the top 3 or 4 inches of soil and replace with fresh mix.

Spring and fall are perhaps the best time to repot plants, but actually, if a plant requires it, repotting can be done at any time of the year.

To remove a plant from a container, rap the sides of the tub or box sharply with a hammer. Grasp the crown of the plant with one hand, the pot with the other hand, and jiggle the plant from side to side. The idea is to ease the plant from the pot rather than pull it out. The root ball should slide from the container. If you have trouble getting the plant loose, keep moving it about in the container to loosen the roots. Do not jerk it out. Repotting is a shock to a plant because roots are torn, the plant is disturbed, and it has to adjust to new conditions.

With very large containers (over 24 inches), it is sometimes necessary to break the pot to avoid pulling out the plant and harming the root structure. This is not a very economical procedure, but generally after years of use the pot is somewhat soiled or rotted and it is time to discard it anyway, or you might want a different kind or color of container.

When the plant is out of the old pot, crumble away old soil and trim dead roots—the ones that are brown or black. Do not take away all soil from the roots; a ball should remain intact as much as possible. Put drainage material in the new container, about 1 inch of pot shards for a 10-inch pot, 2 inches for a 20-inch pot, and so on; set a layer of soil in place. Center the plant; if it is too high in the container, remove some soil. If it is too low, add some soil. Fill in and around with fresh soil. Be sure the crown of the plant is above the soil line, since burying it will cause rot. Fill the container with soil to 1 inch from the top and pat down with your hands to eliminate air pockets. Water thoroughly and then water again so all the soil is thoroughly moistened.

For a nursery-grown plant in a can, water it the day before repotting time. Then slit the sides of the can with a can cutter. (If you have the can slit at the nursery, repot immediately; do not let the plant dry out.) Place the plant on its side on the ground and pry loose half the can; slide the plant out of the can and repot following the directions above.

Do not pick up balled or burlapped shrubs and trees by the stem. Cradle the root ball in your arms and set it in place in the container with drainage stones and a bed of soil. Fill the pot with soil to 1 or 2 inches from the rim. Water thoroughly.

Be sure to soak all old and new containers before using; otherwise the container will absorb water that the plant needs. Simply immerse them in water for a few minutes. Place containers where you want them before you plant them. As mentioned, large tubs and boxes filled with soil are heavy to move.

WATERING AND FEEDING

Water plants thoroughly and deeply and then allow them to dry out before rewatering. Every second month flood the plants to leach harmful acids and salts from the soil. When and how often you water plants depends on the plant and its container. Plants in unglazed containers dry out faster than those in wooden tubs. Large containers hold moisture longer than small ones, and plants close together shade one another and help to prevent excess moisture loss. Ferns and palms like a soil that is moderately moist at all times, while dieffenbachias and philodendrons like to dry out thoroughly before they are watered again.

Although plants need sufficient water, soil should never be allowed to get soggy, for then the air is forced from the soil and the plants suffocate or drown. Occasionally through neglect or circumstance, soil in large containers becomes caked, and it is then impossible for water to penetrate it and get at the roots. Poke some holes in the soil.

Roots constantly take nutrients from soil, and since frequent waterings leach out food faster than we realize, some feeding is necessary for pot plants. However, too often people are anxious to see new growth and feed plants too much. There are times when fertilizing a plant is beneficial, and there are times when it can kill a plant.

Do not feed newly potted specimens for several weeks; there are adequate nutrients in fresh soil. Ailing plants and those resting should not be fed because the roots simply cannot absorb nutrients and will burn. In spring and summer, when most plants are growing, feed them every other watering, but in fall and winter, when many of them rest, do not feed.

There are many kinds of plant foods, some specifically for azaleas or roses, others for different plants. Liquids, powders, or pellets come in bottles, packages, and cans. Read labels before selecting food, and use the fertilizer that is most convenient for your purpose. All fertilizers have nitrogen, phosphorus, and potash in varying amounts marked on the package (in that order). Nitrogen stimulates foliage growth, phosphorus promotes root and stem development and stimulates bloom, and potash stabilizes growth and intensifies color. Give foliage plants a high-nitrogen fertilizer, say 20–10–10; flowering species need less nitrogen because high concentrates of it can inhibit blooming. Select 10–10–5 for flowering plants.

I do not feed cacti or succulents, orchids or bromeliads. Through the years I have found that these plants do better without feeding if they are properly watered and have proper light.

PLANT PROTECTION

If you follow a few simple rules, garden room plants will be relatively free of pests. Good care is the best prevention against trouble of this sort.

Wash foliage every month; this simple step both keeps plants free of insects and makes leaves shiny. Inspect all new plants for insects. If possible, soak the plant to the rim in a tub of water for about an hour; you will be surprised at the unwelcome guests that come to the surface of the soil. Remove infected or infested plants immediately before pests spread to other plants, and isolate ailing ones that you suspect are diseased or have insects.

To eliminate the hiding places of many insects —under pots—elevate the containers on blocks of wood so air reaches the bottom of the pots. Keep plants in a well-ventilated place; stagnant air is an invitation to insects.

For information on insects and ways to avoid them, see Chapter 9.

CHAPTER 6

Orchids

Today thousands of people are growing orchids; this amazing plant family offers incredible blooms of dramatic beauty. Orchids are almost impossible —even for the novice—to kill.

KINDS AND COST

There are many fine orchids that make excellent plants, for garden room or greenhouse, from the purple cattleyas we know as the corsage flowers, and the cymbidiums with their tall spikes of blooms, to the cypripediums (the lady's slipper orchids), in exotic colors. There are also botanicals, or species—orchids pure from the hand of nature. These wild types bloom indoors as they do in their native homes in the jungles of South America or the mountains of the Far East. Plants and flowers come in many sizes, from 1 inch to 6 feet, with flowers as tiny as a dot or as large as a dinner plate.

The cost of orchids is minimal when you consider the pleasure they give. A mature plant, that is, a plant that has already bloomed once, costs from $5 to $10, and there are enough varieties of these moderately priced orchids to supply you for years (and they will live for years, too). You can get plants from local dealers or from mail-order specialists.

ORCHID CARE

Generally, there are two kinds of orchids; terrestrial (earth growing), which grow the same way as garden plants, and epiphytic (airborne). The terrestrials grow in soil as most other plants do. The epiphytes, which make up the majority of orchid species, cling to tree branches. Both types require a somewhat different container than standard plants. The orchid pot has slots at its side to permit circulation of air around the roots (this is especially important for epiphytes because they are basically air plants). You also need a potting mix and osmunda fiber, or use fir bark, the chopped bark of various evergreens. These packaged materials are sold at nursery centers. Remember to use fir bark as it comes from the package, but soak osmunda overnight so it will be easy to work with when potting.

To make sure of drainage (for water must not linger at the roots), break up some old clean flower pots and use them as shards at the bottom of the pot. (Pour boiling water on the pots and shards to make sure they are really clean.) Fill each pot a third full with these broken pot pieces. Then set the orchid plant in place and fill in and around with osmunda, bark, or the mixture for terrestrials. Press the material down with a short piece of blunt wood and work the material from side to side to the center until you have filled the pot firmly to within ½ inch of the rim. (Leave this space to receive water.) Water the plant moderately at first.

I put newly potted plants in shade; in a few weeks I move them to a bright or sunny place, depending on the plant's needs. Start a regular watering schedule once plants are in place.

Since orchids require a great deal of air circulation around the pot and plant, I suspend orchid

Diacattleya 'Chastity,' a
favorite hybrid orchid
with shell-pink blooms.
(Joyce R. Wilson)

Although Ansellia orchids come from
Africa, they are right at home in
garden rooms, and provide dramatic
color.
(Jack Kramer)

Small flowers but lots of them make
Rhyncostylis orchids popular with
growers.
(Jack Kramer)

containers from wires in the ceiling. In this position they enjoy the best of light, and they are attractive to look at because they are at eye level.

Don't let anyone scare you by saying that orchids are temperamental as regards watering or humidity. If you are negligent and forget to water orchids for a few weeks, they will survive better than most plants, and an average humidity of about 40 to 50 percent suits most species. Temperature need not be a prime concern; most orchids will thrive at 70 to 80 degrees F. during the day and 50 to 60 degrees F. at night.

There are cool-growing orchids and warm-growing types, but separate growing areas are really not necessary. I have grown coelogynes from the Andes Mountains alongside species from Burma. Indeed, orchids are so tenacious that they will adjust to their environment after a few months. Do not panic if they lose leaves and do not fare too well during the adjustment period; eventually they will be capable performers indoors.

I am frequently asked how to water orchids. The answer is not how to water the plants nor how much water, but *when* to water them. Generally, orchids like to be flooded and then allowed to dry out before being moistened again; however, do not let them get bone dry. Some orchids, like dendrobiums and lycastes, must be completely dry for about a month before and after flowering. Herein lies the key to success with orchids: *Observe their resting periods.* In the plant descriptions that follow we mention resting times.

Some orchids require a great deal of sun—laelias, cattleyas, vandas—while many orchids such as coelogyne and phalaenopsis prefer and must have a rather shaded spot. They need light but never sun. Place your orchids in the greenhouse with great care; an inch one way or the other can make all the difference in the world. If a plant does not respond on the shelf after a few months, move it to a hanging basket suspended from the ceiling. If a basket orchid is not faring well, move it to another place; placement of plants is vital to successful orchid growing.

EASY-TO-GROW ORCHIDS

Here are seven easy-to-grow orchids; a complete compendium of orchids follows this list:

1. *Brassavola nodosa,* the lady-of-the-night, is treasured for its delightful evening scent and the beauty of its pale-green flowers marked with red. Give this small plant full sun with plenty of water all through the year. Flowers can appear at any time, as the plant wills.

2. The Cattleya hybrid is showy and dramatic because of its 3- to 4-inch flowers of rose-purple with yellow throat. Give this 15-inch plant full sun and plenty of water when it is growing. There are many other Cattleya hybrids. Some are equally easy to grow, some are more difficult.

3. *Cycnoches chlorochilon,* the swan orchid, bears the largest flowers of all—a full 7 inches across—and they are fragrant. The long, graceful, curling column is chartreuse; the lip is creamy white and dark green. Blooms, in lovely abundance, appear in summer. When the leaves are fully open on this 12- to 24-inch plant, let the soil get quite dry, to encourage budding. As the flower spike starts up from the base, resume watering. Then, after the flowers fade, give the plant a 4- to 5-week dry rest. Undemanding, this orchid can be grown successfully at any light window.

4. *Lycaste aromatica,* the cinnamon orchid, has a spicy scent. The brilliant orange-yellow flowers are a joy in winter. This 12-inch plant will thrive at any light window, but give it a 3- to 4-week dry rest, both before and after flowering. It sheds leaves at the time of blooming or just afterward; this is natural and not a sign of ill health.

5. *Odontoglossum grande,* the tiger orchid, is a brilliant sight with its large, vivid yellow and brown-barred flowers. Grow in full sun but keep rather cool at night—about 60 degrees F. if you can manage it—and water only moderately. The lavish flower show is staged in winter on these 15-inch plants.

6. *Oncidium ampliatum,* a 12-inch plant, is adorned in early spring with a spray of hundreds of bright yellow, red-spotted flowers. Keep the bark absolutely dry for 5 to 7 weeks after flowering, but during this period mist the foliage from a house-plant sprayer about once a week. Water heavily from August through November, when it is in active growth.

7. *Saccolabium curvifolium,* also known as *Ascocentrum curvifolium,* provides a colorful show from April to June. The erect spikes, several to a well-grown plant, are crowded with 20 to 30 flow-

Vandas are handsome orchids with long-lasting flowers; this is Vanda 'Evening Glow,' an excellent garden room subject (top, left).
(Jack Kramer)

The tulip orchid, Anguloa, always causes comments in a garden room, for it is a stellar plant in bloom (top, right).
(Joyce R. Wilson)

Lycaste gigantea is a dramatic orchid with flowers that last many weeks.
(Jack Kramer)

ers. This small plant from Thailand needs some sunlight and moderate moisture all year. It does best in a 4-inch pot of fir bark.

OTHER ORCHIDS TO GROW

Included here are some of the orchids I have grown for many years in my garden room. Many of them are dendrobiums, for they are so rewarding and give a harvest of spring and summer flowers. In fall and winter they need little care other than reduced moisture and cool temperatures. Epidendrums are favorites as well, for they, too, require so little care and yet bloom religiously every year. Most of these plants are large and offer excellent decoration at ceiling height in baskets or on shelves.

In shady areas of the garden room I concentrate on coelogynes and zygopetalums, which offer a bounty of winter color, and ever-popular paphiopedilums (lady's slipper orchids) and catasetums, always desirable in any indoor scene.

COELOGYNE. Cool-growing epiphytic orchids with pendant scapes of white, beige, or green flowers. Grow plants in fir bark kept evenly moist except as noted below. Give bright light but little sun, and provide 40 to 60 percent humidity.

C. cristata. Three-inch crystal-white flowers in winter; needs rest after blooming.
C. massangeana. Dozens of 1-inch beige flowers in fall; no rest needed. Spectacular as basket plant.
C. speciosa. Three-inch beige flowers in winter; no rest needed.

DENDROBIUM. A genus of striking epiphytic orchids with cane growth and large flowers. Leaves are leathery and some of the prettiest species deciduous. Plants need a southern or western exposure; pot in fir bark and water heavily when plants are growing; rest plants with little water in late October for about 4 to 6 weeks at 50 to 55 degrees F. to encourage budding. After they flower, rest plants again with little moisture for about 6 weeks; return to warmth.

D. dalhousieanum. Evergreen with tawny yellow flowers with crimson markings; spring or early summer bloom.
D. moschatum. Deciduous; musk-scented, large yellow-rose flowers from spring to August. No rest needed.

D. pierardi. An easy-to-grow deciduous plant with handsome 3-inch pink flowers on long pendant scapes. Rest after blooming.
D. thyrsiflorum. A magnificent evergreen orchid with white-and-gold flowers in April or May. Rest somewhat after blooming.

EPIDENDRUM. Free-flowering, mostly epiphytic plants with two types of growth: cane-stemmed or with pseudobulbs. They bear handsome flowers in shades of pink, red, yellow, or white. Grow plants in fir bark; give full sun. Keep cane-stemmed ones moist all year but rest the others for about 5 weeks before and after flowering.

E. atropurpureum. Resplendent with dozens of 1-inch brown and purple blooms in early spring.
E. cochleatum. This one has dramatic dark-maroon and chartreuse seashell-shaped flowers on and off throughout the year.
E. lindeyanum. Cane growth; rose-purple bloom with white lips, in fall.
E. nemorale. Three-inch rose-mauve flowers in summer. Needs rest after blooming.

MILTONIA. Popular orchids with large, open-faced flowers, usually white or red or shades of red, that stay fresh on the plant for months. Pot in fir bark; keep moist but never wet. Give bright light, little sun. Many brightly colored hybrids available.

M. candida. Chestnut-brown and yellow flowers in the fall.
M. flavescens. Yellow sepals and petals; yellow lip marked purple; blooms appear in summer.
M. vexillaria. This one has lovely lilac-rose flowers in spring.

PAPHIOPEDILUM. These terrestrial orchids easily adapt to indoor growing and produce flowers in glowing colors; some like warmth, others thrive in coolness. Give them a shady place and keep the potting mix (equal parts of soil and shredded osmunda) moist all year.

P. callosum. With marbled foliage and 2-inch pale-green and rose flowers, this lady's slipper blooms from winter to spring. Needs coolness.
P. fairieanum. Nodding yellow and purple flowers on long stems make this orchid desirable, and it is so easy to grow. Likes coolness.
P. philippinensis. A glossy green-leaved species with multicolored exquisite flowers on tall stems.

VANDA. A genus of epiphytic orchids with handsome, flat-faced flowers in an incredible variety of colors. With straplike growth, plants can grow to 8 feet. Give vandas full sun and plenty of water during the growing season. Use large-grade fir bark, and do not repot the plants too often. Once every 3 or 4 years is satisfactory.

V. cristata. A medium-sized plant that blooms on and off throughout the year with lovely green and maroon flowers.

V. roxburghi. This one has 2-inch pale-green flowers splotched with brown, the lip lined white with a violet-purple disc.

V. sanderiana. The famous vanda well known throughout the world, *V. sanderiana* (and its many hybrids) has 5-inch flowers, soft pink color suffused with white, lower petals generally with red veins.

V. rothschildiana. Here is the splendid blue vanda with dazzling 6-inch flowers in winter. This species prefers coolness to thrive.

ZYGOPETALUM. Growing in the ground or in trees, this is a fine group of orchids that generally like coolness and shade. The plants produce exotic flowers in colors of blue and green, often laced with brown markings. These orchids need a shredded osmunda and soil mixture; repot only when absolutely necessary.

Z. crinitum. A pendant flower scape bears green flowers barred with brown, the lip a startling purple. Winter flowering.

Z. mackayi. A large plant with plicate foliage and stunning 3-inch flowers; sepals and petals are green blotched with brownish-purple, lip white and purple and beautifully scalloped.

CHAPTER 7

Greenhouses and Greenhouse Mechanics

The greenhouse was originally a place to protect plants from weather. The plants were notably fruits (primarily oranges, although cherries, plums, and pineapples were also grown). The first structures had movable wooden shutters on a wooden frame; the shutters could be removed by day and replaced at night. The rooms were called *orangeries* and had high ceilings and large windows on the south, with pans of hot water or flues behind the walls for heating. Thus greenhouses were cumbersome and utilitarian rather than attractive.

When flat glass became available in the eighteenth century, panes of it replaced the shutters. That was the age of Linnaeus, the great plantsman, and tropical plants, including orchids, were imported in great numbers. These plants were erroneously designated as hothouse plants that needed stagnant humid conditions to survive, and soon glass-sealed greenhouses came into being, one more elaborate than the next. At the same time, the conservatory was born; its structure was similar to the greenhouse's, and the difference between the two buildings was not entirely clear. However, generally the conservatory (also called *solarium*) was attached to a building or house and used to *display* plants, rather than to grow them.

Greenhouses are classified as commercial or amateur (hobby greenhouses). The former, infrequently seen, are rarely aesthetically pleasing, since they are one monotonous glass peak after another. The amateur greenhouse, which is extremely popular, is generally a lean-to building attached to the house. No longer used essentially as a housing for fruits, as in former times, today's greenhouse is more an extension of the home. This double role has somewhat confused greenhouse nomenclature, but basically the greenhouse is a structure in which plants are *worked with* rather than displayed.

Once greenhouses were only for the wealthy, sealed enclosures to protect exotic plants that no one else had. Today greenhouses are for everyone and for all sorts of plants. A complete 5′ by 3′ by 8′ by 7′ prefabricated unit with heater, vents, and growing benches costs as little as $800, a small cost for the large amount of exciting gardening that awaits the possessor of one. Flowers in winter, seed sowing, grafting, and air layering are only a few of the possibilities with a garden under glass.

Architecture has changed through the years, and so have greenhouses. They are no longer stereotyped, aluminum-and-glass structures rectangularly shaped; they are unique buildings in all shapes and sizes, including one structure that revolves with the sun's rays.

Because there are so many kinds of greenhouses, choose wisely; know what kind of greenhouse you want and where it will go, to ensure pleasure. Decide just how much time and space you can devote to gardening. Send for greenhouse manufacturers' catalogs to get you started; survey the field before you make a choice. Most people buy commercial prefabricated units, but you may decide to build your own greenhouse.

KINDS OF GREENHOUSES

Manufacturers have responded enthusiastically to the public demand for gardens under glass. But

While conventional greenhouses are popular, several companies now offer the glass house in varying designs. These have proved satisfactory where something different is wanted. *(Sturdi-Built Mfg. Co.)*

while the design of the greenhouse has changed and prices have become feasible, the actual construction of the greenhouse—putting it together—still must be done by the buyer, or he must hire professional help.

The basic greenhouse styles are called freestanding, attached, or lean-to. The lean-to is perhaps the most popular; as the name implies, it is attached to your residence, garage, porch, or patio. It comes in several different sizes, with a curved- or straight-eaved roof, and may be a glass-to-ground structure or have a waist-high foundation wall. The advantages of the lean-to are that it is close to the house, so you can enjoy your plants even in inclement weather and water and electrical lines can easily be connected to the house supply without exorbitant cost.

The freestanding greenhouse is a detached, self-supported glass structure that has two sides and two ends, with a door at one end. This type of unit is best for the professional grower rather than the average gardener. Its cost can be high, since heat, water, and lighting facilities must be extended some distance from the residence. The structure resembles a commercial grower's greenhouse, although recently some hexagonal and round designs have appeared that are more eye pleasing.

In addition to the standard glass and aluminum greenhouses, there are various plastics used in the construction of greenhouses. Polyethylene film is a flexible plastic in 2-, 4-, or 6-mil thickness and may be used to cover a greenhouse frame temporarily. However, it will not last more than a few months before replacement is necessary.

Mylar or polyester plastic is flexible and lasts longer than polyethylene, but it is rarely aesthetically pleasing and lasts at the maximum about 2 years. Fiber glass is a rigid plastic, flat or corrugated, made under several trade names. It comes in different colors and sheet sizes and does away with the breakage factor associated with glass. However, it scars and weathers with age and is not a lifetime material.

Greenhouses are sold prefabricated, which means in pieces. As mentioned, you still must put them together or hire someone to do it. This is not as easy as it sounds, for even in large cities there are few professionals available to install your greenhouse. When I decided on a particular greenhouse for my Northfield, Illinois, home (twenty miles from Chicago), I could not find anyone to install it. The contractor had put in the foundation and a slab floor, but the actual construction of the house finally fell to a carpenter. Although instruction sheets are as clear as the manufacturer can make them, the actual piece-by-piece installation frequently confuses nonskilled people.

WHERE TO PUT THE GREENHOUSE

Although many manufacturers recommend a southern exposure for a greenhouse, I have seen lovely glass gardens on the east and west sides of a house. And even with a northern exposure you can grow splendid foliage plants and many of the shade-tolerant orchids. But do not put a greenhouse in a place that is completely shaded by trees; all plants need light, even though not all need direct sunlight.

A southern or southeastern exposure is recommended because the greenhouse benefits from winter sun. An eastern exposure is good because it gets morning sun. A greenhouse facing west will have only bright light and late afternoon sun.

Be sure that the type of greenhouse you select will blend in with the architecture of the house, and, if it is a lean-to, will look like part of the house rather than merely a tacked-on structure.

Many housewives prefer the growing area to adjoin the kitchen, and this is certainly a good idea because it offers a lovely view of greenery from the kitchen window. Greenhouses placed adjacent to the living room are popular, too, and even the intimate glass garden next to a bedroom has its merits. Many bathrooms are also incorporating greenhouse niches. The garden has invaded the house, and it is welcome. The possibilities of where to put the glass garden to make it part of the living scheme are many, so select the location carefully. Give up the idea of putting the greenhouse on the sunny side of the house if it will add more interest to a different area.

FOUNDATIONS

In the excitement of selecting your greenhouse, do not forget the foundation for the structure, for a suitable foundation is necessary as a support. The foundation is a masonry wall partly underground, partly above grade level. It may be poured concrete, brick, or concrete blocks. The foundation must extend to frost level or a few inches below the frost line. Frost lines must be observed for foundations; building codes require it. In Illinois the frost line is 48 inches; call your local building-code department to find out the frost line of your area.

Furthermore, a solid foundation will prevent cracks and crevices from forming in the structure (alternate freezing and thawing of the ground can cause walls to crack). If you live in a climate that is temperate year round there are greenhouses that set at ground level and require no foundation; they rest on concrete slabs or shallow footings.

Greenhouse prices do not include foundations or footings. You can, of course, install them yourself, but because it is hard you might want to hire a professional. A foundation for a 16′ by 20′ greenhouse costs about $600, but this varies from state to state.

Once the foundation walls are in place, it is time to frame the greenhouse; if you have purchased a prefabricated unit, the next step is to lay out all the pieces and start putting them together. As I've mentioned, instruction sheets leave some guesswork, so it is best to hire someone with a knowledge of building to help you with the project. The frame will, in most cases, be made of aluminum, although West Coast manufacturers use redwood. Either material is satisfactory, the difference being more in appearance than in performance. However, aluminum is permanent, brings down the cost of maintenance, is easy to work with, and is designed so that there is no condensation drip from the sash bars. Painting is not necessary, as it is with wood, and weather will not affect aluminum.

CONTROLS

Greenhouse controls for heating, cooling, ventilating, and watering facilities are as important as the building itself. The prime purpose of a greenhouse is to provide controlled conditions for plants, so select the best climate-control systems you can afford. Then you can enjoy growing plants without worrying about weather.

The greenhouse and its working controls must be considered first, before any plants are selected, before any actual growing is done. Heaters, ventilators, and so forth are all part of the initial expense and should be considered beforehand.

How to heat your greenhouse is generally the first question that confronts new owners. There are several kinds of heaters: electric; warm air, gas fired; or warm air, oil fired. What you choose depends on several factors and is discussed in the next section. Ventilation goes hand in hand with heating, so the proper facilities to ensure fresh air must be incorporated in the greenhouse. These controls may be manually operated or completely automatic ventilating systems. The type of watering devices must also be considered; are you going to hand-water everything, or would a master-control watering system be better? Shading of glass, work areas, and places for plants—benches, shelves—are other necessary components of greenhouse growing.

HEAT

If you plan to enjoy your greenhouse year round, some form of heating will be necessary. Even in southern climates, small electric heaters or gas units must be kept in operation during chilly nights. Of course, the colder your winters the more heating is necessary to maintain good plant health.

Once greenhouse heating was a maze of pipes and problems, and only hot-water heat was considered satisfactory. Today's greenhouse heating systems are sophisticated, and warm-air systems are considered as good as the hot-water types. Installation and operation of the heating unit is not too difficult, but determining what kind of heating fuel to select—gas, oil, or electricity—can be tricky.

Several factors determine the right heating system: the size of the greenhouse, its location, and the kind of plants you want to grow. Fortunately, manufacturers' catalogs supply much technical data to help you. Before you select the heating system, check the gas and electric rates in your area. Decide which will be the most economical and then investigate specific systems.

The ratings of various heaters are determined by estimating the British thermal units (BTUs) required to adequately maintain the night temperature you want in the greenhouse. Choose a heater that gives more than the minimum BTUs necessary for minimum night temperature. This extra safety margin is necessary in case your area has high winds or if you decide later to increase the growing area.

Freestanding greenhouses are rarely seen today;
properties are much smaller than years ago.
(Lord & Burnham)

TYPES OF HEATERS

The warm-air, gas-fired heater is quite popular for hobby greenhouses; one type requires a chimney, but another does not. A compact space heater for the average greenhouse of 12' by 18' has a safety pilot and thermostatic control. You will have to provide some type of masonry or metal chimney so that harmful fumes will be dissipated safely outside the greenhouse. Another unit is a nonvented heater that does not need a chimney; the combustion chamber is sealed and outside the greenhouse. This heater extends only about 10 inches into the greenhouse and needs only a 17" by 20" wall opening. Both types of heaters are approved by the American Gas Association (AGA).

The warm-air, oil-fired heater is small enough to install under a greenhouse bench. It has a 100,000-BTU output, which is sufficient for the average-sized greenhouse, and a gun-type burner, blower, two-stage fuel pump, and full controls. You must use a masonry chimney or a metal smokestack about 24 inches above the ridge of the roof.

Electric heaters are satisfactory for small greenhouses. They can be installed easily, are automatic, and are equipped with a built-in circulating fan and a 40 to 80 degree F. thermostat. Separate heavy-duty electric lines are necessary, and the heater and thermostats should be installed by a professional in accordance with local electric codes.

A hot-water heating system that can be installed in the greenhouse or in an adjoining area is also available. It provides automatic, forced-circulation hot-water heat.

Some people use a heating extension kit to attach into a home furnace, but this is rarely a satisfactory method because most home furnaces are not equipped to handle the extra load. The better method is to have an individual heater for your greenhouse. However, if you decide on your home furnace for greenhouse heat, be sure the BTU of your present boiler has a sufficient capacity for the extra output. A plumber can advise you.

VENTILATION

Good ventilation will provide relief from heat during the day, help control such disease problems as mildew, supply fresh air, and ensure good humidity. Because hot air rises, the logical place for vents is along the ridge of the greenhouse. However, vent sashes on the sides of the greenhouses are satisfactory, too, and provide cross ventilation. When the vents are open, warm air flows out to cool the greenhouse and at the same time provides fresh air for best growing conditions.

Greenhouse ventilation used to be a manual job. A flat metal push-rod raiser was elevated to the proper height, where it was pushed over a protruding device, thus holding the vent open. Other manual apparatuses were the arm and rod, and rack and pinion types, each operated with gears. A chain ran from the lower gear to one attached to the horizontal rod at the top of the greenhouse. Elbows were attached to the sash, and pulling on the chain activated the gear that opened the sash. With either method you had to operate the ventilators, and this was tricky sometimes.

Certainly automatic ventilating equipment is the answer. Although it may cost more at the start, in the long run it pays for itself. A moisture-proof thermostat set at the proper temperature regulates the opening and closing of the ventilating sash. When the greenhouse becomes too warm, the sash opens automatically; when the proper temperature is reached, the sash closes. The thermostat is protected from direct sun and warm air blasts from heaters. The unit is generally placed at bench line, or may be suspended from the electric conduits by a roof bar.

WATERING SYSTEMS

Automatic-control watering systems are certainly a convenience for commercial growers, but their use in home greenhouses is limited because different plants require different amounts of water and usually at different times. Thus an automatic perforated hose system operable from one faucet is of questionable value. Yet, for people who grow annuals and perennials, overall watering can be a convenience, since it is simply a matter of turning one faucet to water all the plants.

Watering systems operated by various devices are available, as are time-clock control systems that turn water on and off at a predetermined time. These systems are connected to your water supply; just set the clock.

This elegant garden room brings the outdoors indoors with great
flair. The ceiling design is intricate and beautiful.
(Rohm & Haas)

A garden room can also furnish an intimate eating area; this redwood-and-glass structure has a concrete aggregate floor.
(Joyce R. Wilson photo; Andrew R. Addkison, Interior Designer)

This garden room at the rear of the house is resplendent with color; house plants decorate the inside of the room (Dizygotheca in the right corner), while outdoor flowers frame the area.
(Max Eckert)

Lean-to greenhouses are popular;
they fit into almost any situation.
This curved-eaved model is functional
and attractive.
(Lord & Burnham)

Somewhat different from the lean-to
greenhouse, but still attached to
the home, is this small glass house,
a veritable treasure of plants.
(Lord & Burnham)

SHADING

In many parts of the country, direct summer sun causes greenhouses to heat up considerably and burns plant foliage. Most plants cannot tolerate full summer sun; they require light to grow but not direct sun, so some means of shading is necessary for the greenhouses. There are many shading materials. Some are simple to install, others are more elaborate.

The old-fashioned paste or powder whiting can be applied with a sprayer or paintbrush. A gallon of white paste mixed with gasoline or benzine covers about 600 square feet of glass. The paint is usually applied in spring and is generally applied again in summer. Paint comes in white or green and is available as paste or powder. This material is cheap, but application is time consuming and with rain the paint becomes unsightly.

Aluminum slats or wood panels are a far more attractive answer to the shading problem. They cost more than pastes or powders, but they are made in sections to fit the glass panels of most greenhouses and give a better appearance. The aluminum panels come in kits and can be easily assembled; the wood panels are simple to install, too, and once up can be left in place all summer.

Roll-up wood shades are perhaps more practical than panels or slats. They are an attractive means of shading, and can be lowered or raised as needed, which is a definite convenience on cloudy days when plants still need light.

Plastic shading (flexible, light-green 8-mil sheet film) is also used as shading for greenhouses. Somewhat better-looking than whitewash, it comes in 29-inch widths and 25-foot lengths. Plastic shading reduces sunlight transmission considerably and can be easily installed to the inside of the glass panes. Cut the plastic to the exact size of the glass, then moisten the glass with a hose or a sponge and place the sheet of plastic against the inside glass. Smooth it down as you would wallpaper with a squeegee or a brush. Get rid of all air bubbles; the surface tension of water between glass and plastic will hold the shading in place. In early fall, when shading is no longer needed, the shading is easy to remove. Simply loosen the corners of the plastic sheets and peel them from the window.

CHAPTER 8

Advantages of a Greenhouse

To me, the greenhouse is a place to work with plants and enjoy nature firsthand. You can grow flowers for cutting, you can sow seeds to get a head start on spring, or you can have herbs and vegetables. You can relieve the tensions of the day by working with nature, and you can save money.

GROWING PLANTS FROM SEED

The gardener who grows his plants from seed garners more than economic advantages. He can have the most recently introduced plants, sometimes in the first year. Some, of course, may not be too good, but certainly there will be a few really exciting new kinds. I still remember the joy of having the first dwarf red impatiens in full bloom long before they were available to the public.

Secondly, by growing from seed you can enjoy the old favorites that are getting lost in the shuffle because of the increasing production of new hybrids. A friend gave me some seeds of a forgotten species of iris, unavailable commercially, that had been growing in her garden for fifty years. And, finally, many times the color of flower or variety of vegetable that you want is not available at your local garden center, so growing plants from seed in the greenhouse makes it possible for you to have what you really want and not what you must buy.

Expensive or elaborate equipment is not necessary for growing seeds in the greenhouse, nor is a knowledge of botany. All you need is a love of nature and that certain curiosity that is part of everyone's makeup.

GETTING STARTED

Generally, you will buy seeds from suppliers. And there is a harvest of beauty to be found in the seed catalogs available from many of them. The catalogs are a joy to ponder because you don't have to wait to see what the nursery will or will not have next year. Today's seeds are better and vastly improved over seeds of even last year, and new varieties appear frequently.

After you have made your seed selections, decide what soils, containers, and so forth you want to use. New growing mediums and containers are available at suppliers. Perlite is a good growing medium, and milled sphagnum moss represents a tremendous advance in seed-starting techniques. Vermiculite is another good medium that I use frequently.

Seed starting has become infinitely more fun, too, with Jiffy peat pots and flats, Poly-trays, and new seed pellets and tapes. These ingenious devices make seed growing so easy even a child can do it.

Thus there is little excuse for the greenhouse gardener not to have his own plants from seed. Using all these new techniques (according to directions), and having the proper lighting and the right ventilation, will guarantee you success in seed growing.

Ferns and orchids blend effectively in a quiet, sun-shafted corner.

(Morley Baer)

Seed-starter kits are now available from growers and make growing plants from seed easy and almost foolproof.

(George Park Seed Co.)

SEED CONTAINERS AND GROWING MEDIUMS

There are many seed containers, some professional and others homemade. Suppliers carry starting kits, transplanting pots, plant mediums, and so forth. Just what kind of container you use depends on your personal taste. For years, the packing boxes (flats) for window glass have been my favorites. These range from 12′ by 18′ to 24′ by 30′ in size, are 3 to 4 inches deep, and already have drainage space between the boards. Such boxes are still available from glass dealers in some cities, free for the asking.

Household items such as coffee cans, aluminum and glass baking dishes, plastic cheese containers, and the aluminum pans that frozen rolls come in also make good seed containers. Make sure that any household item you use as a container is at least 3 inches deep and has some drainage facilities (punch tiny holes in the bottoms of pans). Also remember that in aluminum and plastic housings the planting mix will dry out quickly, so water more frequently.

For the beginner I suggest using standard clay pots from nurseries. They are inexpensive, always look neat, and hold enough moisture so that frequent watering is not necessary. Ask for azalea pans—squatty pots—which are now available in several sizes.

Other suitable containers include the galvanized metal pans sometimes found in used furniture shops or the custom-made ones from metal shops. Be sure they have drainage holes.

The kind of growing medium you choose depends to a great extent on the plants you want to grow. I have found that a peatlike mix is excellent for cactus and succulents, but use standard vermiculite and milled sphagnum for annuals and perennials. For starting trees and shrubs I use equal parts of sphagnum, perlite, peat moss, and vermiculite.

You can mix your own materials or buy them packaged. In any case, select a sterile medium, or otherwise the soilborne fungus known as "damping-off" can occur. Good growing mediums are:

Milled sphagnum. This is an old-timer and a good starting medium that generally gives good results. Its disadvantage is that it has to be carefully watered to maintain an evenly moist bed.

Perlite. This is a volcanic ash that does not absorb moisture readily. However, it holds moisture within itself, providing a moist growing medium.

Mixed with a little sterilized soil it provides a good medium; by itself it has a tendency to float and disturb the seed bed.

Vermiculite. Vermiculite is expanded mica that holds moisture a long time; I use it and get excellent results. It is sold under various trade names, and lately I have seen it packaged with added ingredients, which may or may not be a good idea (I have not tried it yet).

Many gardeners prefer a mixture of equal parts vermiculite, sphagnum, and perlite, which is a light, clean, and easy-to-handle medium I highly recommend.

Steer clear of packaged soil mixes because they are generally too heavy for successful seed sowing. But if nothing else is at hand, use it in combination with some finely porous, sterile soil.

CUT FLOWERS

When gray days get you down, there is no better tonic than walking into your greenhouse and cutting some flowers for indoors. This is indeed a convenience, and growing blooms under glass is easy with controlled conditions.

For a continuous supply of flowers, place the plants directly in benches filled with soil. Although carnations and chrysanthemums are always a favorite for bench growing, snapdragons, asters, calendulas, and alyssum are also fine possibilities, and there are dozens more.

Prepare your soil bed with care; this and watering is almost all you have to do to have splendid flowers. Make benches from wood, or buy commercial ones. In any case, fill the bench first with a copious layer of drainage material—shards or pebbles. Then fill the bench with a good potting soil; you want a rich soil to get plants to grow quickly.

Put the seedlings in place. (The seedlings can be plants you started yourself from seed in the greenhouse or ones you have bought from a nursery.) Do not water too much at first; keep the seedlings just barely moist. Keep the humidity at about 50 to 60 percent to encourage good growth. Try not to grow too many different kinds of plants at first. Try a few, such as snapdragons, and stock together in a bench the first year. The following year grow several kinds. In time you will gain actual know-how experience and your home will have cut flowers all year round.

Because there are so many cut flowers for green-

Opening off the recreation room, this greenhouse
affords room for plants and at the same time
makes the area attractive.
(Molly Adams)

house growing, it is impossible to offer a comprehensive list; here are some favorites to try:

Ageratum
Aster
Buddleia
Butterfly flower (Schizanthus)
Chrysanthemum
Delphinium
Marguerite
Marigold (Tagetes)
Nasturtium (Tropaeolum)
Pansy
Phlox (annual)
Snapdragon
Statice
Stock
Sweet pea
Zinnia

STARTING PLANTS FOR OUTDOORS

As I've mentioned, besides being economical, growing plants in a greenhouse is an excellent way to stock the garden; for you know what you have, and there is a great reward in looking over your landscape and knowing *these are your plants*. Start the seeds as described earlier in this chapter.

The following plants are ideal for starting in a greenhouse and getting a head start on spring.

Anchusa capensis
Ageratum houstonianum (flossflower)
Antirrhinum majus (snapdragon)
Arctotis stoechadifolia grandis (African daisy)
Calendula officinalis (pot marigold)
Centaurea cyanus (cornflower)
Cleome spinosa (spiderflower)
Cobaea scandens (cup-and-saucer vine)
Cosmos bipinnatis
Dimorphoteca aurantiaca
Gaillardia pulchella (annual)
Godetia grandiflora
Gypsophila elegans (annual)
Helichrysum bracteatum (strawflower)
Impatiens balsamina (balsam)
Linum grandiflorum
Lobelia erinus (annual)
Matthiola incana (stock)
Myosotis alpestris
Petunia hybrids

Phlox drummondii (annual phlox)
Reseda odorata (mignonette)
Salpiglossis sinuata (painted tongue)
Scabiosa atropurpurea (pincushion flower)
Tagetes erecta (African marigold)
T. patula (French marigold)
Thunbergia alata (black-eyed Susan vine)
Verbena hortensis (garden verbena)

VEGETABLES AND HERBS

If you have the space, grow some vegetables and herbs in addition to plants. Your own vegetables are a fabulous bounty, especially during the bleak days of winter, and herbs for salads and stews—fresh from the greenhouse—are impossible to buy. It is not necessary to have a lot of vegetables, and space will probably prohibit it anyway, but a few carrots, beets, and tomatoes are always welcome.

The joys of vegetable growing far outweigh the care you have to give the plants. Most vegetables grown in greenhouses—tomatoes, radishes, carrots—need only a good lightweight soil that drains readily and plenty of sun. Keep the plants well watered after the seedlings have been put in their permanent locations and provide a buoyant humidity, of about 50 percent.

Tomatoes can be grown in large tubs. In fact, there is now a tomato variety that is especially developed for container growing. Grow plants to a single stem and stake them for support or it will be impossible to handle them. Polinate blossoms by hand or use a hormone-type tomato spray on the blossoms.

Bibb lettuce will grow in the same temperature (60 degrees F.) as tomatoes and needs only an even soil and some sun. Carrots and beets need cooler growing conditions, about 45 to 55 degrees F.

You can start herbs from seeds or buy them as seedlings at nurseries; you may not want too many to start. A few selected herbs such as basil, dill, sweet marjoram, tarragon, and a few chives may be all you need for your cooking purposes.

Most herbs do fine with plenty of sun and a minimum temperature of 50 degrees F. Soil should be rich and drainage near perfect. Provide adequate humidity and good air circulation and mist the plants occasionally to keep them in tip-top condition.

Here is a small greenhouse that was crafted by the
homeowner for his geranium collection.
(Jack Kramer)

CHAPTER 9

Techniques of Greenhouse Gardening

Growing plants under glass is somewhat different from growing plants in the garden or tending a few houseplants. In the greenhouse—if ventilation and heating facilities are installed properly—plants are under almost ideal conditions and grow better and faster, so they require more nutrition and feeding.

All the cultural aspects of gardening must be understood by the greenhouse owner. Watering, humidity, feeding, and pest control are prime considerations in the greenhouses if you want healthy plants—and who doesn't? These cultural aspects are not difficult to master, but some knowledge of soil and humidity, temperature, and ventilation is necessary. Experience will do the rest.

SOIL FOR PLANTS

Soil is the building block of all plants—it supplies water and nutrients to the roots and supports the plant. A good growing mix is essential for plants, and each gardener, after a time, will discover a favorite soil recipe that suits most of his plants. Recipes for soils are numerous, and although I recommend some balanced growing mediums in this chapter, they are not mandatory.

The ingredients of the soil mixture may vary, but one factor remains constant: the consistency of the soil. This is as important as its fertility. Soil must be porous in texture so it can retain water long enough to benefit the roots, but not so long as to cause them to rot. If the soil is too sandy, water will run through it quickly without benefiting the plant. On the other hand, if soil

is heavy it remains wet, so oxygen cannot reach roots and plants soon die.

Organic matter is the stuff that good soil is made of. Well-rotted leaves and vegetable matter (humus or compost) are the prime ingredients of a good potting soil. They provide nutrients for plants and keep soil porous. You can buy humus by the sack or compost it yourself in a backyard bin.

The soil mix I use for most plants in the greenhouse is the same one I suggest for the garden room:

1 part garden loam
1 part leaf mold
1 part sand

For plants such as African violets and ferns add 1 part peat moss to the mix. Add sand for cacti and succulents. Use fir bark or osmunda for orchids and bromeliads (as is discussed in Chapter 6).

Soil bought by the truckload or in a package or bushel from a florist may or may not be pasteurized (sterilized). Pasteurization gets rid of insects, harmful bacteria, and weed seeds. The process can be done in the kitchen oven: Fill a pan with garden soil and bake for 45 minutes at 180 degrees. Let the soil cool completely and stir it before you use it for plants. Be ready for a rather unpleasant pungent odor if you sterilize your own soil.

I have found soil sold by the bushel at florists' shops to be my best all-purpose mix, and it is generally sterilized. Soil purchased in sacks from florists rarely has been satisfactory for most of my plants; invariably I add essential ingredients.

Aphids are another plant pest and once they get a foothold they can ruin a plant: eliminate them quickly for they multiply rapidly.
(USDA)

Mealybug is a common plant insect; the best way to avoid having pests attack plants is to observe plants frequently and catch trouble before it starts.
(USDA)

Packaged soil is generally too heavy and much of it is exorbitantly expensive.

PLANT FOODS

Plant foods, like soils, are numerous; these preparations are added to the soil to stimulate plant growth. Feeding is not necessary when you use new, fresh soil. It is only after the plants have depleted the soil of nutrients (a month or more) that fertilizing is beneficial. Until then, a good potting mix will contain adequate food for the plant; excess feeding will only harm it.

Nitrogen, phosphorus, and potash are the three basic ingredients of soil. Fertilizers contain these elements in proportions, listed, in the order above, on the package. Thus, as I've already mentioned, a 10–10–5 fertilizer contains 10 percent nitrogen, 10 percent phosphorus, and 5 percent potash. Filler materials make up the remaining 75 percent.

Nitrogen, perhaps the most important ingredient, promotes healthy green foliage and stimulates growth. Phosphorus promotes good root growth and helps to encourage flowering. Potash builds up resistance to disease. Trace elements—iron, boron, manganese, etc.—are also necessary for healthy plant growth; they are included in most fertilizers.

Feeding solutions are generally beneficial to most plants; however, a few plants, like orchids and some ferns, resent feeding. Success with additional feeding of plants depends on when you feed plants and other factors. For example, never feed freshly potted plants—they don't need it—or those in parched soil; fertilizers can burn plant roots. Feed more in spring and summer, when plants naturally grow, than in fall and winter. Do not fertilize ailing plants or newly transplanted seedlings.

Try not to set up a rigid feeding routine. It is much better to observe each plant and decide whether to feed it. Overall heavy drenchings of plant food can harm plants.

If you use plant foods on a regular basis you will have to be sure to leach plants at least once every 6 weeks to drain away excess salts that can accumulate in the soil and harm the plant. (Leaching, as I've said, is flooding the plant with clear water several times.)

WATERING

How much water to give plants always seems to confuse people, but it shouldn't. If conditions are ideal, with temperature, humidity, and light in balanced proportions, most plants can use a great deal of water. When you water your plants do it thoroughly, and then allow them to approach dryness before you water them again. Scanty waterings will cause pockets of dry soil in the container, and the roots will be hindered.

Overall watering rules are impossible to give for all plants. The size of the container, the plant itself, and the greenhouse conditions dictate just how much water a plant needs.

TEMPERATURE AND HUMIDITY

Humidity and temperature go hand in hand with watering and ventilation to keep plants healthy. Temperatures that soar during the heat of summer days will not harm plants if the humidity is kept high. At night, plants need a normal drop in temperature (about 20 degrees F.) and much less humidity.

Although many greenhouse manufacturers recommend a cool or warm house for plants, I have found that most plants can be grown in a moderate-warm house, that is, 70 to 85 degrees F. by day and 58 to 65 degrees F. at night, with a relative humidity of about 50 percent. Avoid too much humidity, because, coupled with gray days, it is an invitation to fungus diseases.

INSECTS AND DISEASES

Insects and plant diseases are no longer a scourge for greenhouse gardeners. New methods of growing, resistant plants, and better controls now make these minor problems.

If culture, watering, light, and feeding are good, and humidity, temperature, and ventilation are satisfactory, the insect problem in home greenhouses is virtually eliminated. However, few gardeners are perfect, and there may come a time when insects invade the greenhouse or disease strikes a plant. There is no need to panic, nor is there any need to run out and buy a barrage of

Powdery mildew is a disease that
causes premature falling of leaves.
Low temperatures and cloudy days are
an invitation for this disease
to start.
(USDA)

Virus disease attacks plants too;
this is rose mosaic. Fortunately,
virus disease rarely occurs in the
small greenhouse.
(USDA)

chemicals to fight the invaders. First know what you are fighting before you do battle.

Many times, what appear like insects may simply be poor culture. Spraying with insecticides would be futile, and might harm the plants. Here are some signs that indicate poor culture rather than insects:

1. A plant with spindly growth or one that wilts. Temperature or light is not to its liking.

2. Foliage withers. This may be caused by a draft directly on the plant, a drastic change in temperature, or watering with icy water.

3. Leaves with dry areas. Usually caused by impurities in the air or industrial fumes.

4. Leaves with burned or scorched areas. Direct sunlight magnified by a defect in glass can act like a magnifying glass and burn leaves.

5. Buds that fail to open. Usually caused by a dry atmosphere or too much sun.

What to Look For

Aphids, red spiders, and mealybugs are generally the insects that do the most damage to greenhouse plants. Occasionally leaf miners and leaf rollers, sow bugs and plant bugs may attack plants, too. In any case, if detected early none of these pests should cause havoc.

Aphids are plant lice. They are pear shaped, have soft bodies, and may be green, black, or red. They multiply quickly and can swarm all over a plant, causing spindly and deformed foliage.

Red spiders, or spider mites, are microscopic spiders that gather on the undersides of leaves. They weave a fine web and cause leaves to become brown and drop off. They thrive in a stagnant situation.

Mealybugs are oval insects covered with what looks like cotton. They gather on stems, leaves, and the undersides of leaves and harbor their young in leaf axils. These insects suck the plant sap, and foliage and flowers become stunted.

Scale insects are hard-shelled, readily seen pests that attach themselves to leaves or stems. Foliage will turn pale as these insects suck the juices from a plant.

Thrips are tiny yellow, brown, or black insects that move quickly. A heavy attack leaves foliage streaked and silvery.

Slugs and snails are easy to see. Although they are not true insects, they are quite bothersome because they eat holes in foliage. They do their work at night and generally hide during the day.

Preventatives

If you are against using poisons for gardening, there are many old-fashioned remedies for eliminating insects. In fact, some of these methods work better than poisons and save the cost of spray or dusting equipment and cleaning paraphernalia. Most important, they eliminate the hazards of keeping poisonous materials in or near the home.

Wash a plant thoroughly with a hose or spray strongly to eliminate aphids. A solution of 1 tablespoon of alcohol to 1 quart of water applied with a small brush will do the job, too. A mixture of soap and water often deters red spiders, and mealybugs can be eliminated with a solution of equal parts of water and alcohol followed by a washing with soap and water and a rinsing with clear water. Or go over a plant with a Q-Tip dipped in alcohol. Gently scrub off scale with a stiff brush dipped in soapy water.

Cut potatoes in half and lay them on the soil to lure snails and sow bugs to the surface, where you can destroy them. Beer works well, too: put a small amount in a bottle cap and leave it overnight in the greenhouse.

Insect traps and light traps are other good precautions against bugs in the greenhouse. So are natural repellents, which are inexpensive and easy to use. The repellent may be chemical or physical. Wood ashes will keep some types of insects away from plants, as will a nontoxic material called acrylin resin. The odor of tar paper will repel insects. Oil of cloves and camphor will thwart most ants, and oil of citronella is a good insect repellent. Ground pepper is also effective in keeping some insects away from plants.

You can also use organic preparations or those containing rotenone, quassia, or pyrethrum. These are nature's own insect repellents and are now being used in commercial insecticides. They are nonpersistent and do not harm warm-blooded animals.

If old-fashioned remedies do not work or if organic repellents fail to control specific pests, use a group of synthetic chemicals known as organic phosphates (these are quite effective and relatively safe). Malathion is the leader, and, al-

Good soil is the basis of good plant growth; soil should feel porous and mealy in the hand.
(USDA)

A brick foundation wall makes this greenhouse appear to be an integral part of the house. Note the special shading slats
(Aluminum Greenhouses, Inc.)

though it is often used to control a host of insects, it is really only effective against certain ones. Dibrom is another organic phosphate that has proved to be valuable to the gardener. Diazinon, the most toxic, is being used a great deal lately and is effective against many insects. It is said to break down in 10 to 12 days. However, all these solutions are still poisonous, so use them with discretion.

The most convenient kinds of insecticide are called *systemics,* and are used in granule form. Apply systemics to the soil and then water the soil. One application will protect most plants (but not ferns or palms) from the majority (but not all) of sucking and chewing insects for 6 to 8 weeks.

Plant Diseases

Treat plant diseases—blight, canker, mildew —with fungicides or cultural controls. To prevent disease from ever starting in your greenhouse, give plants space to grow and always be sure some air is moving through the growing area. Cloudy days coupled with lingering moisture are an invitation for disease, so water sparingly, if at all, on prolonged gray days.

Blights of various types sometimes attack flowering plants, causing petals to fall away and flowers to rot. Control by using captan or zineb dusts twice weekly as flowers open.

Black spot is another bacterial disease. It causes black spots on foliage and is sometimes bothersome to chrysanthemums. Use captan or ferbam.

Botrytis or petal blight attacks snapdragons, chrysanthemums, and other flowers. It is a brownish-gray mold that appears on the plant. Control with captan or zineb.

Damping-off is liable to attack any seedling; it is a rotting of the plant tissue at the soil line. Control by steam-sterilizing the soil.

Powdery mildew often attacks flowering plants. The sign is a white powdery film on stems and leaves. Control with karathane.

Rust causes spots on foliage and can attack carnations, asters, etc. Use captan.

Mosaic or ring spot viruses are other bacterial diseases, but, fortunately, they are not often seen. Plants affected with these viruses develop brown or yellow rings with dwarfed leaves. There is no known control for this disease, so it is best to destroy infected plants.

Alocasias are fine greenhouse plants with dramatic
leaves; they like a moist humid atmosphere.
(Hort-Pix)

CHAPTER 10

Foliage and Flowering Favorites for Greenhouse Conditions

If your greenhouse is crowded with bedding plants, herbs, or vegetables, you will still want some pot plants, either as accents to create a lush green feeling indoors or as hobby plants. Although there is a tremendous choice of foliage favorites (philodendrons, dieffenbachias, and ficus), I generally use them in the garden room only. In the greenhouse I grow the lesser-seen green plants: alocasias, caladiums, crotons, and marantas. These plants offer a wealth of interest.

Grow these plants under approximately the same conditions: 70 to 80 degrees F. by day and about 60 to 68 degrees F. at night, with an average humidity of 40 to 50 percent. For the most part, protect the plants from direct sun because they thrive in a bright but somewhat protected area.

ALOCASIAS

Alocasias are exotic plants from Borneo, Australia and southeastern Asia. These well-grown plants, with their heart-shaped leaves and prominent veins, are a dramatic sight. Some alocasias have purple foliage, and others are brownish green or olive green. The veining is white, pearl gray, or red. Although most alocasias grow to 30 inches in height, smaller dwarf types have recently been introduced.

The plants should be grown in peat moss, perlite, and some humus, and good drainage is vital. Alocasias require constant moisture at the roots at all times and revel in warmth, with a minimum 62 degrees F. at night. Keep them out of the sun, but give them some bright light. Provide 30 to 50 percent humidity and wash the leaves occasionally with a damp cloth.

Still somewhat expensive, alocasias are now available at florists' shops. Here are some I have grown in the greenhouse.

Alocasia amazonica. Handsome hybrid, with dark-green, white-veined foliage.
A. cuprea. Waxy maroon-purple leaves with prominent veins; compact growth.
A. johnstonii. Foliage marked with red veins.
A. lowii grandis. Deep brownish-green leaves.
A. lowii veitchii. Arrow-shaped, mottled leaves.
A. sedenii. Hybrid with olive-green and silver foliage.
A. waveriana. Dark-purple lance leaves, with purple edges.
A. zebrina. Rare; mottled stems.

CALADIUMS

Caladiums are spectacular in full leaf in summer. The leaf color ranges through shades of pink, red, white, or green marked with deeply etched veins of contrasting color. The foliage has a papery texture and the leaves are pleasingly arrow shaped. These are impressive plants.

In their native land, the jungles of Colombia, caladiums have a distinct wet and dry season. You can start the tubers in spring for summer show or plant them in early fall for winter decoration.

Start the plants in equal parts of sandy loam and peat moss. Keep them warm (minimum of 70 degrees F.), and place them in bright light.

Geraniums are always lovely to add color to a scene.
(Merry Gardens)

Caladiums are easier to grow than most people think; they come in an array of splendid colors and freshen any greenhouse.
(George J. Ball, Inc.)

Water them scantily for the first few weeks, but once growth starts increase moisture and feed them moderately every 2 weeks. When caladiums start their dormancy, decrease moisture and store the tubers in a warm, dry place for the following spring.

Good varieties of caladiums for you to grow in the greenhouse are:

'Appleblossom.' Transparent appleblossom-colored foliage, green border.

'Bleeding Heart.' Heart-shaped, pointed leaves marbled white, green, and red.

'Debutante.' White and green leaves with a rosy central area.

'Edith Mead.' Small dark-green and white leaves, red veins.

'Gail Dee.' Pink, mottled light- and dark-green foliage.

'Jacqueline Gireaud.' Yellow-green leaves splashed with crimson.

'Lord Derby.' Quilted rose-pink, green-veined leaves.

'Maid of Orleans.' Deep-green leaves marbled pink.

'Pink Blush.' Crinkled carmine-rose leaves with thin dark-green borders.

'Red Chief.' Lance-shaped leaves, red with green border.

'Southern Belle.' Rose-pink leaves, green edges.

'White Christmas.' Pure white, deep-green-veined leaves.

CROTONS

Crotons are sun-loving plants that have bright-colored foliage. The leaves come in a veritable rainbow; combinations of yellow and green are perhaps the most common colors. However, there are also plants with foliage of bronze, copper, pink, and purple. Some leaves are broad, while others are lance-shaped and scalloped. And several forms of crotons have narrow leaves or leaves that grow in a spiral pattern.

Native to the humid tropics, crotons revel in warmth and humidity, and the soil in which they grow must be kept constantly moist. Many will survive in less sunlight than in their natural land, but they cannot tolerate drafts and sudden changes in temperature.

Grow the plants in equal parts of loam, sand, peat moss, and leaf mold. Place a few chunks of charcoal in the pot to keep the soil sweet. Pot in small containers rather than large ones, and remember that these plants need plenty of water to prosper.

Red spiders are fond of crotons, so wash plants weekly with a damp cloth to avert attacks. Do not spray foliage with insecticides; the plants are highly susceptible to poisons and can be harmed by chemicals.

Here are some ideal croton varieties:

'Applause.' Large semioak leaves, yellow and green to pink.

'Cameo.' Brilliant shell-pink foliage.

'Columbeona.' Carmine-purple and green leaves.

'Gloriosa.' Red-purple and maroon leaves.

'Harvest Moon.' Green leaves with yellow and white veins.

'Jungle Queen.' Red, pink, and maroon leaves.

'Monarch.' Broad irregular leaves; brilliant red.

'Spotlight.' Narrow irregular leaves; green, yellow, and red.

'Sunday.' Large semioak foliage; orange, yellow, and red.

MARANTAS AND CALATHEAS

The marantas are decorative plants native to the South American jungles; and although the family is not large (only about 200 species), it is confusing in its nomenclature. The group also contains calatheas and ctenanthes. No matter how they are listed in catalogs, and it will vary, these are superlative foliage plants. The leaves have a crinkly texture and are beautifully marked in olive-green or brown with undersides of magenta purple. These fine plants thrive in a shady place; however, do not put them in total darkness and expect them to live.

Keep the soil a bit on the wet side during the summer, evenly moist the rest of the year. The plants like warmth (never less than 58 degrees F. at night), and require 30 to 50 percent humidity. Give them a porous soil of 2 parts peat moss, 1 part sand, and 1 part loam. A few species are dormant in winter, so keep these almost dry at that time.

You may have to search for a few of the species

described here. Only popular ones are being offered by nurseries, but I'm sure we will see more of them in the near future.

Calathea argyrala. Silver-gray and green.
C. concinna. Dark-green leaves with feather design.
C. insignis. Light-green with olive-green markings.
C. lietzei. Light green leaves, purple underneath; feather design.
C. makoyana. Olive-green, pink, silver, and green foliage. Outstanding.
C. ornata. Roseolineata. Pink on white stripes. Striking.
C. o. 'Sanderiana.' Dark, waxy foliage heavily marked with shades of green.
C. veitchiana. Iridescent leaves.
C. zebrina. Dark, velvety purple leaves with chartreuse markings.
Ctenanthe 'Burle Marx.' Gray-green, dark-green leaves.
C. oppenheimiana. Silver and green.
Maranta bicolor. Flatter design; dark-green, grayish, and green.
M. erythreneura. Bright red veins on pearl-gray background.
M. leuconeura 'Massangeana.' Pearl-gray-green foliage.

FLOWERING GEMS

For bright color and cheer on winter mornings, flowering plants are everyone's favorite. There are thousands of choices for greenhouse growing, but perhaps gesnerads, geraniums, and begonias are the favorites. These plants offer almost year-round color and add the finishing touch to a hobby greenhouse.

Gesneriads

African violets have been popular for years, but it is only recently that other gesneriads have become popular. In this overlooked group there are some stellar plants with flowers as pretty as, or perhaps prettier than, African violets. Kohlerias, laden with brilliantly colored, bell-shaped flowers, are stunning. Gloxinias, so easy to grow in a greenhouse, are floriferous and exciting plants. Smithianthas, columneas, and achimenes are only a few

of the many other gesneriads. We shall discuss many; we are omitting African violets not out of preference but merely because of space. (There are many fine books on these plants.)

Like orchids, many gesneriads come from the tropics, but this does not mean that they must be grown in excessive heat and humidity. Most are comfortable if you are, and average greenhouse conditions suit them well.

Some gesneriads—achimenes, kohlerias, smithianthas—have a scaly rhizome at the base of the stem. Others, like rechsteinerias and sinningias, have tuberous roots that act as water-storage vessels, and still others have fibrous roots.

Filtered or bright light is best for most gesneriads. Use a loose, well-drained soil of equal parts peat moss, leaf mold, garden loam, and sand. Pot the plants carefully; perfect drainage is vital to successful growing. During growth, these plants require plenty of water. Tepid water is best because cold water shocks the plants and causes the leaves to become spotted. After flowering, most gesneriads rest; when they do, place them in a cooler area, about 50 to 65 degrees F., and keep the soil barely moist. At all times provide adequate moisture in the air for these plants; 30 to 40 percent will ensure healthy growth.

In the last few years, hybridists have made amazing progress with this family of plants, and new and beautiful varieties are introduced frequently. Don't miss these flowers; they really show.

Achimenes 'Blue Star.' Pale- to dark-blue flowers with white eyes.
A. 'Charm.' Floriferous, coral-pink blooms.
A. 'Dazzler.' Small ovate leaves; large red flowers.
A. 'Leonora.' Dark-green foliage; violet-purple blooms.
A. 'Violetta.' Dark-green leaves; almost purple flowers.
Aeschynanthus lobbianum. Shiny dark-green leaves; scarlet blooms.
A. pulcher. Green leaves; scarlet flowers.
A. speciosus (lipstick vine). Orange flowers; shiny green leaves.
Columnea arguta. Trailing vine with pointed leaves; red flowers.
C. hirta. Three-inch orange blooms; vining growth.
C. microphylla. Long-trailing stems with button leaves; burnt-red flowers.
C. 'Stavanger.' European hybrid with bright red blooms.

C. 'Canary.' Cornell hybrid. Upright growth; yellow blooms.

C. 'Cornellian.' Floriferous, orange flowers.

Episcia acajou. Silver foliage; red flowers.

E. cupreata. Hairy copper leaves; red blooms. Many forms.

E. lilacina. Bronze leaves; blue flowers.

E. 'Yellow Topaz.' Green foliage; yellow flowers.

Kohleria allenii. Hairy leaves; red and yellow flowers.

K. amabilis. Velvety green leaves; pink flowers with purple dots.

K. bogotensis. Speckled leaves; red and yellow blooms.

K. eriantha. Bright-red tubular flowers.

K. hirsuta. Hairy foliage; red blooms with pale throat.

Rechsteineria cardinalis. Small, green, and velvety leaves; scarlet tubular flowers.

R. leucotricha. Large leaves covered with silver hairs; coral blooms.

R. macropoda. Bright-green leaves; small red flowers.

Sinningia 'Buell's Blue Slipper.' Velvety foliage; blue flowers.

S. 'Defiance.' Large leaves; dark-crimson flowers with waxy edges.

S. 'Emperor Frederick.' Upright, dark ruby-red blooms bordered with white.

S. 'Emperor William.' Large leaves; violet-blue flowers, white border.

S. 'Pink Slipper.' Light-green leaves; rosy-pink flowers with dark centers.

S. 'Switzerland.' Soft leaves; scarlet flowers edged with white.

Smithiantha cinnabarina. Nodding scarlet-red flowers.

S. multiflora. Soft, hairy plant with white blooms.

S. zebrina. Leaves covered with silky hairs; red flowers.

S. 'Golden King.' Golden-yellow blooms.

S. 'Orange King.' Orange-red flowers.

S. 'Rose Queen.' Rose-pink flowers.

Streptocarpus rexii. Pale-blue flowers; many forms with pink, blue-white, or purple blooms.

S. saxorum. Dark-green leaves; white and lavender flowers.

Geraniums

Geraniums, correctly called *pelargoniums,* offer almost constant color if given full sun and grown in the cool end of the greenhouse. Plant them in a rather firm soil mixture of 3 parts loam to 1 part sand, plus a little peat moss. Water freely, then let dry out a little before watering again. Geraniums bloom best when potbound, so use small pots. Martha Washingtons and the ivy-leaved varieties rest somewhat in winter; water them moderately then, and do not feed. Feed the others every other week when they are in active growth, which is most of the time if the weather is sunny.

Avoid overwatering geraniums, do not put them in high humidity, and do not mist the foliage.

ZONALS. These are the familiar old-fashioned types with scalloped leaves and brilliant single or double blooms. Most varieties grow to 30 inches; there are also dwarfs and miniature forms.

'Better Times.' Red flowers.
'Dreams.' Double salmon-pink.
'Flare.' Single salmon-pink.
'Harvest Moon.' Single orange.
'Patricia Andrea.' Brilliant rose color.
'Salmon Irene.' Double, one of the five Irenes.
'Snowball.' Double white.
'Summer Cloud.' Double white.

MARTHA WASHINGTON OR LADY WASHINGTON GERANIUMS. These make a colorful spring display in the greenhouse. Flowers are two- or three-color blends, whites tinged with lavender or pink, vibrant reds and deep purples. There are also small, free-blooming pansy types. Cut the plants back after flowering and always grow in the coolest part of the greenhouse (45 to 55 degrees F.).

'Dubonnet.' Ruffled red-wine.
'Easter Greeting.' Cerise flowers.
'Gardener's Joy.' Blush-white with rose markings.
'Lavender Grand Slam.' Deep tone and compact grower.
'Madame Layal.' Purple and white pansy type.
'Springtime.' Ruffled white with rose-colored throat.

IVY-LEAVED. Fine plants with trailing stems, glossy ivylike foliage, and cascades of flowers, these are excellent for baskets in the greenhouse. Pinch the plants in late winter or early spring to encourage many shoots to grow.

'Charles Turner.' Fine double pink.
'Comtesse de Grey.' Single light-pink.
'New Dawn.' Double rose-cerise.

Pendula Begonias are favorites too;
ideal for basket growing in the
greenhouse.
(Jack Kramer)

Begonias are other greenhouse
favorites.
(Joyce R. Wilson)

Begonias make any greenhouse
sing with color; this is a multiflora
begonia 'Helen Harms,' bright
yellow.
(Antonelli Bros.)

'Santa Paula.' Double lavender-purple.
'Victorville.' Double dark-red.

Scented-leaved geraniums, and fancy-leaved types are other members of this large plant family, that is so popular with gardeners all over the world.

Begonias

Begonias come in such an incredible variety that you will certainly want to try some in the greenhouse. There are all kinds, and it seems each group contains stellar plants. Angel wings are laden with cascading bowers of flowers; rhizomatous begonias—those with gnarled, handsome stems—offer an infinite variety of leaf textures and colors. The cascading begonias for baskets are always a joy to see, and the hirsute group are forever interesting. And the majestic rex begonias, with leaves that remind you of brilliant tapestries, are ideal.

Although begonias are often considered shade plants, this does not mean that they will grow or bloom in dim light. In fact, most begonias need as much sunshine as possible in winter to be at their best. Rhizomatous types will tolerate a somewhat shaded place, but even they prefer bright light for maximum growth.

Use a good, porous potting soil for the plants; they like almost perfect drainage and will do fine in average greenhouse temperatures—that is, 70 to 80 degrees F. during the day and 58 to 62 degrees F. at night. For rhizomatous begonias I use 3 parts loam, 1 part coarse sand, and 1 part rotted leaf mold. To an 8-inch pot I add 1 tablespoon of bone meal and granulated charcoal. All other begonias I plant in 3 parts loam, 2 parts peat moss, 1 part leaf mold, 1 part well-rotted manure, and 1 part sand. Bone meal and charcoal are also added to the mix. Rex begonias, which like a very porous mix, are planted in 2 parts leaf mold, 1 part top soil, and 1 part sand.

Although it is true that overwatering may kill begonias, if all other cultural factors are good—soil, potting, light—a thorough soaking followed by a drying-out before watering the soil again is the best procedure. The roots have time to absorb all moisture, and, if they are somewhat dry for a day, there is little harm done. When to water depends on many variables: weather, pot size, location, and the plant itself, but there are still some general rules to follow.

Large pots of soil hold moisture longer than small ones, and begonias in 10- or 12-inch containers will only need water once or twice a week in winter; increase the watering schedule in spring and summer to 3 or 4 times a week, and then reduce it again in fall. Smaller begonias in 4- to 6-inch pots will need more water. Some of the old-fashioned ways of determining when a plant needs water are still valid. Feel the soil; if it is dry and crumbly to the touch, water. Lift the pot; dry ones weigh less than moist ones. Tap the side of the pot. If it has a hollow ring, water the plant. Remember to water plants thoroughly. Really soak them until excess water drains from the container.

Begonias respond beautifully to feeding and should have fertilizer when they are actively growing, usually in spring and summer. In cold weather, when many begonias are dormant, do not feed them at all. Moderation is the rule with feeding. Use a 10–10–5 commercial soluble plant food, applying half the dosage recommended on the package. Do not feed newly potted plants, because there are enough nutrients in the soil to sustain the plant for at least 3 months. And do not feed ailing plants, because the roots generally cannot absorb moisture and nutrients.

Repot begonias infrequently; large plants in 10- to 12-inch containers can go 3 years without being disturbed. Smaller plants will need semiyearly repotting. For the most part, begonias are not troubled with insects, although occasionally aphids or mealybugs may be a problem. Household remedies as described earlier will eliminate the pests.

Listed below are some begonias from each group to try in the greenhouse. These are the ones I have grown and found to be very satisfactory. It is by no means all the kinds of begonias you can grow; if these become your favorite plants, by all means experiment and grow many.

HIRSUTE BEGONIAS

Begonia 'Alleryi.' Old-time favorite; frosted green leaves accented with purple.

B. fernando costae. Low-growing, almost stemless plant with fleshy cupped leaves.

B. hugellii. Tall and stately species; bright green leaves, red underneath.

B. 'Loma Alta.' Red plush leaves make this one an exceptional species. Grows easily with little care.

B. metallica. Handsome dark-green, purple-veined foliage accented with silver hairs.

B. scharffiana. Robust hairy plant; large olive-green leaves.

ANGEL WING AND OTHER FIBROUS BEGONIAS

Begonia acutangularis. Lovely, pointed, ruffle-edged green leaves make this one desirable.

B. 'Alzasco.' Dark-green, silver-spotted leaves. Easy to grow.

B. 'Di-Erna.' Blooms freely; lovely coral flowers.

B. 'Grey Feather.' Slim and arrowlike leaves, dark green, almost gray; white flowers with a pink tinge.

B. maculata. Somewhat temperamental; lovely silver-blotched foliage and pink blooms.

B. 'Sylvan Grandeur.' Heavily textured foliage with pink spots; bright-pink blooms.

RHIZOMATOUS BEGONIAS

Begonia 'Beatrice Haddrell.' Small star-shaped leaves, almost black in color, with green veins; pink flowers.

B. 'Bessie Buxton.' Upright grower. Dark-green foliage; pink blooms.

B. 'Crestabruchi.' Unique plant with heavily ruffled yellow-green leaves.

B. 'Erythrophylla' (beefsteak begonia). Round leaves, green on top and red underneath; fine pink flowers.

B. 'Maphil.' Sometimes called B. 'Cleopatra.' Often classified as a hanging basket plant, although it is not a true trailer. Exquisite foliage splashed with golden chocolate-brown and chartreuse coloring.

B. dayi. Light-green foliage with red veins; ivory flowers on long stems.

B. mazae. Round bronze-green leaves; light-pink blooms.

B. 'Ricky Minter.' Handsome variety with dark bronze-green ruffle-edged leaves.

OTHER BEGONIAS

There are so many varieties of rex and tuberous begonias that it is impossible to suggest superior plants. They come in many colors and sizes, one prettier than the other, and they are generally listed by color rather than by varietal name because there are so many. With this group of begonias, choose the colors you like the best and start from there.

See Chapter 6 for orchids.

Where to Buy Plants

Most large cities have florists that carry specimen size or decorator plants, and new companies are opened occasionally. Thus, the list that follows is merely a sampling of suppliers, and no doubt the yellow pages of your phone book in your local city will turn up other sources for large plants.

Alberts & Merkel Bros., Inc.
P.O. Box 537
Boynton Beach, Fla. 33435

Everett Conklin & Co., Inc.
Montvale, N.J. 07645

Fantastic Gardens
9550 Southwest 67th Avenue
South Miami, Fla. 33030

Fennell Orchid Co.
26715 Southwest 157th Avenue
Homestead, Fla. 33030

Julius Roehrs Co.
East Rutherford, N.J. 07073

Kendra Studios, Inc.
125 North Wabash Avenue
Chicago, Ill. 60602

Max Schling, Seedsmen, Inc.
538 Madison Avenue
New York, N.Y. 10022

The Greenery
243 East 53rd Street
New York, N.Y. 10022

The Greenhouse
254 East 51st Street
New York, N.Y. 10022

Greenhouse Manufacturers

Aluminum Greenhouses, Inc.
14615 Lorain Avenue
Cleveland, Ohio 44111

Metropolitan Greenhouse Mfg. Co.
1851 Flushing Avenue
Brooklyn, N.Y. 11237

J. A. Nearing Co., Inc.
4229 Bladensburg Road
Brentwood, Md.

Pacific Coast Greenhouse Mfg. Co.
650 Bayshore Highway
Redwood City, Calif.

Redfern's Prefab Greenhouse Mfg. Co.
3482 Scotts Valley Drive
Santa Cruz, Calif.

Sturdi-Built Mfg. Co.
11304 Southwest Boones Ferry Road
Portland, Ore. 97219

Texas Greenhouse Co.
2717 St. Louis Avenue
Fort Worth, Tex. 76110

Books to Read

Blake, Claire L. *Greenhouse Gardening for Fun.* New York: Barrows, 1967.

Crockett, James Underwood. *Greenhouse Gardening as a Hobby.* New York: Doubleday, 1961.

Kramer, Jack. *1000 Beautiful House Plants and How to Grow Them.* New York: Morrow, 1969.

Potter, Charles H. *Greenhouse, Place of Magic.* New York: Dutton, 1967.

Taylor, Kathryn S., and Gregg, Edith W. *Winter Flowers in Greenhouse and Sun-Heated Pit* Rev. ed. New York: Scribners, 1969.

Wheeler, E. and Lasker, A. C. *The Complete Book of Flowers and Plants for Interior Decoration.* New York: Hearthside Press, 1957.

Index

Page numbers in **boldface** type refer to illustrations.

72 73 74 75 10 9 8 7 6 5 4 3 2 1